PRAISE FOR *THE WAY*

"This is an outstanding book whether you are involved in the sports world or not. While is it autobiographical, telling GSP's personal story through his voice and the voices of the key people in his life, at the heart of it *The Way of the Fight* is about setting and achieving goals, and what it takes to overcome obstacles to become your most successful self. St-Pierre's perspective as a true martial artist (in his way of being as well as by profession) is unique, and his candor is admirable and refreshing. And his dedication to the ongoing battle against bullying speaks to the quality human being he is. I highly recommend *The Way of the Fight*."

—*New York Times* bestseller Tami Hoag

"Like St-Pierre, this book is part philosophical, part scientific, part business-tutorial and even part self-help, with carefully selected pieces of the fighter's personal story interwoven throughout. It's all fascinating, coming from one of the most evolved fighting minds the sport has ever produced. St-Pierre the martial artist dissects MMA on a different level and the layers of dedication he has for his craft are, at times, staggering to read about."

—Loretta Hunt, *Sports Illustrated*

"An interesting view into the psyche of an athlete that can be both charming and outgoing while maintaining his distance as his celebrity has grown . . . the varied perspectives give the book and its subject quite a bit of depth and offer the most insightful view to date of a fighter and person that has not only dominated his sport, but has been one of the foundational figures brdging the gap between MMA's community and the greater mainstream sports audience."

—Sherdog.com

"*The Way of the Fight* [is] a more than serviceable entry in the genre that is likeable for all the reasons its author is likeable: it's aware of its audience, willing and able to share wisdom . . . the story it does tell is both generous and charming.

—Jacob McArthur Mooney, *National Post*

THE WAY OF THE FIGHT

THE WAY OF THE FIGHT

GEORGES ST-PIERRE

with Justin Kingsley

wm

WILLIAM MORROW

An Imprint of HarperCollins*Publishers*

In memory of Jean Couture, my first karate teacher,
who opened my eyes to the world of martial arts

CONTENTS

INTRODUCTION

Every Single Morning Takes Root the Night Before | 3

The Idea for This Book | 7

In Case You Don't Have Time to Read | 12

How I Structured This Book | 15

BOOK 1: MOTHER (MAMAN)

17

BOOK 2: MENTOR—THE GROUND BOOK

with Kristof Midoux, Sensei

41

BOOK 3: MASTER—THE TRANSITION BOOK

with John Danaher, Brazilian Jiu-Jitsu Teacher

89

BOOK 4: MAVEN—THE STANDING BOOK

with Firas Zahabi, Coach

149

BOOK 5: CONSCIENCE

with Rodolphe Beaulieu, Manager/Friend

195

Epilogue | 221

Acknowledgments | 227

THE WAY OF THE FIGHT

It's the repetition of affirmations that leads to belief. And once that belief becomes a deep conviction, things begin to happen.

—MUHAMMAD ALI

Every Single Morning Takes Root the Night Before

I n the calm and quiet of darkness, I move across my apartment—through the living room, before windows that look
over the river and into the city. The dark gray and blue waters
flow toward me and past, but only if I pause to look. I rarely ever
do. It disrupts the routine.

I part the blinds and reach for the curtain rods, hung low
beneath an eight-foot ceiling, and check that my hand wraps are
drying. I run my fingers up and down, flattening the fabric. I set
and reset them along the rod so they'll hang down perfectly; so
they'll hang flat and creaseless; so the day's efforts will evaporate.

I move to the washing machine. I empty the contents of my
workout bag. Another load off.

Back by the balcony, I crouch down and place my gloves
before the electric fan, which spins and rotates, left and right,
doomed to starting over. They're lined up perfectly, my gloves,
like soldiers at attention, like pieces from a puzzle waiting to be
placed, like someone wants to take their picture, like geometry
that matters.

I stand and turn back to the entrance to gather my carry-
all bag and fill it for tomorrow. Always tomorrow. Workout
shorts, two pairs. Training shirts, three, sometimes four of them.

Workout shoes. Gloves for the octagon, and then another pair for the ring. Shin guards. An athletic support, more hand wraps and athletic tape. That usually does it.

From the desperately barren kitchen cupboards I choose an empty water bottle. From the refrigerator I select a protein powder, lots of it. Then I exit, having little other use for this part of the home. I leave the bag by the door—aligned with the console table, near my keys, wallet and phone—and head to the bedroom. I walk into the closet and glimpse at the clothes I own. Most of these items are gifts—sneakers and a few suits I keep for public appearances and special events. I recognize myself in the same jeans and the same plain T-shirts I rotate from day to day. A black one, sometimes a white one.

I kneel down to gather a shoe. I catch the glimmer of my first championship belt. It's lying across the ground, in the corner, gathering time. I pick it up—the shoe—and take him and his brother over to the clothes I've folded and placed on a bench, waiting for the morning. Then I brush my teeth and walk over to my bed.

Now I pray.

There's a spirit there, a presence I can feel, and we have these nightly conversations. I know exactly what I want and what I'm asking for. What I'm *hoping* for. Then I lie there, just another shape in the dark. Sometimes, depending on the position of the moon, I see shadows of these other shapes cutting across the wall and ceiling. The outline of a prehistoric shark's tooth, sitting on my dresser. A T. rex statue, growing when pressed against a beam of light. Japanese cutting swords, two of them, hopelessly waiting to be handled.

And I lie there, at least an hour and often two, as implacable thoughts bounce from the shadows into my head and reverberate against my skull.

The torment of night.

Out of the corner of my eye there appears the only meaningful physical object in my life: a unicorn. A porcelain myth, a twisted horn, a symbol of purity left to me by my godmother when she died. A statuette and a few looping scribbles—words she composed about a boy who'll turn into a man, and how she wished she could be there, how she imagines the life he'll live and the girls and dreams he'll chase.

Eventually, rest comes and, finally, sleep.

With light comes movement. Before the alarm has an opportunity to scream, my eyes open, searching aimlessly before my mind awakes. The first thoughts inside my head are that day's training. Where I must go, what time I must be there, with whom I'll be training, my goals for the day. Life is a program now, a schedule, a balancing act etched into my brain. The written schedule I used to refer to is redundant now. I don't even know where it is.

I rise, I brush and I leave—all within five minutes. Sometimes, with a few minutes to spare, I'll eat a bowl of gruel. A holdover from earlier days when nutrition was subject to meager finances.

I'm out.

I take the elevator down to the basement. My big black truck pulls out of the lot on its own. Windows down or up, the sound of hip-hop is surely loud enough to *charm* my neighbors.

Breakfast—lots of eggs with training partners/friends—and then directly to the first workout of the day. It can consist of wrestling, boxing, Brazilian Jiu-Jitsu, gymnastics, sprinting, Muay Thai, karate or a combination of any of the above. It can last an hour or two. In slow motion or at top speed. Then a shower, and another round of food, then rest, including a nap for forty-five minutes to an hour.

Then comes the second workout of the day. It can also take the form of wrestling, boxing, Brazilian Jiu-Jitsu, gymnastics, sprinting, Muay Thai, karate or a combination, and can take an hour or two, in slow motion or at top speed. And then a shower, and *more* food with friends—*always* with friends.

Then the truck takes me home via the same route as the night before. I park and ride the elevator from the garage up to the ground floor. I walk through the lobby and salute the doorman, the only constant hello I get in what otherwise feels like an anonymous building. I walk to the next elevator bank, punch in my floor number, and head up to my little place that's barely halfway to the penthouses. I walk into the apartment, head straight to the washing machine and remove the objects from my bag. I begin to prepare for tomorrow.

Always tomorrow.

The Idea for This Book...

... first came to me on the day I realized I was going to need major surgery. I chose that day for a reason, and it's a really simple one: because from that day onward I would be inventing the rest of my life. In eight months of surgery, recovery, therapy and training, I would define the new version of me and leave my old shell behind. I would put into practice everything I'd learned in the past three decades, and incorporate new knowledge from the people and the world around me.

In other words, I would be attempting to prove everything I say in this book.

What this means is that I'm laying the groundwork for guaranteed success even before I know the outcome of my return to the octagon.

How? By facing my own fears, by setting a clear goal, by working toward it with all the mental and physical effort possible, and by accepting the result no matter what happens. You see, the outcome of my next fight is not determined in the octagon. It's determined in the weeks and months before the fight, when I'm getting ready for it.

In my loss to Matt Serra, my pride hurt me. When he connected with a good head shot, I should have backed off and got my wits about me, but I didn't. I couldn't believe what was happening to me. My ego didn't like it. Instead, all I could think was, *Wow, I've been rattled by this little guy. Wow, I can't let that happen. I need to get him out RIGHT NOW!* So the real mistake was pride. Getting hit with a good shot should not have been a surprise, and it wouldn't have been if I had prepared for it.

As Aristotle wrote a long, long time ago, and I'm paraphrasing here, the goal is to avoid mediocrity by being prepared to try something and either failing miserably or triumphing grandly. Mediocrity is not about failing, and it's the opposite of doing. Mediocrity, in other words, is about *not trying*. The reason is achingly simple, and I know you've heard it a thousand times before: what doesn't kill you makes you stronger.

* * *

My goal here is to write the greatest book ever written, including these words about fear. It doesn't make any difference that this happens to be the first book I've ever written. What matters most is the spirit in which it's being written—and, quite simply, that it's *being* written. The purpose is to become the best writer in my category (yes, page for page *and* pound for pound). I'm just not sure what the category is yet, and I'm not sure I should care.

The reason behind writing this book is that I'd like to find a way to tell you my story in a different way than it has already been told. In a way, my life can be explained through mathematics and equations. It's really simple: from the moment I started learning and acquiring knowledge, I realized how much there was left to learn. About fighting. About diet. About love and life. About fear! About dinosaurs, even.

So the equation works like this: the more I learn, the less I know. Yes, more is less. That's the way it works in my mind. And it applies to all of us, not just me. For me, that's the secret to a big part of my life and how I became who I am.

Let me explain.

When you learn something—like how to make chili, for example—you acquire some *real* knowledge. Which ingredients to pick, how to prepare the meat, what order to place things in the pot, and how to use a secret ingredient. What happens, though, is that while you learn how to cook the beef and add the ingredients and put everything in the pot, you realize something: there is so much more to learn about cooking. There are so many other combinations for preparing the same meal. Some vary because of the cook, or the country, or the ingredients, or the taste.

So proportionally, even though you learned something new, you realize there is so much more you still don't know about cooking. Therefore, you know less than you knew before.

MDs and PhDs live by the same rules: the more they learn about their field, the more they realize there is left to know. The good ones realize the beauty of this mystery, and they persist. What I try to do is put myself into as many learning situations as possible. When I see something new that I think I'll like, I research it and see if and where I can fit it into my life.

That's why I started doing gymnastics, for example. I'm sure there are a lot of MMA guys and fans who think it's stupid and wimpy to do gymnastics. At least *I* used to think that way. I disregarded gymnastics and believed it was for other people. I was closed-minded.

The key for me is being open to the learning that comes from other sports. To me, seeking knowledge is like opening doors. The planet we live on is a succession of doors. And I know the doors are everywhere. As I grow older, I also happen to be rather aware of my astounding ignorance, and so I've come up with my own cure for a closed mind: try it once, and see.

The first thing I do, and it sounds simple, is figure out how to open one of the doors at a time. Let's say the door is Brazilian

Jiu-Jitsu. The first door you open is stance, figuring out how to hold yourself upright. Once you open the door just a crack, you get to look and peek at what's hiding behind it. You'll get a first glimpse at what's right there within your reach. Maybe it works for you or maybe not, that's part of the deal. But know that it doesn't have to open very far to trigger a reaction.

It's all about curiosity. Sometimes you open the door wide and see right away that the knowledge there does not interest you. This happens to all of us, and it's okay. For example, though I need to eat often and focus on healthy foods in my line of work, I know I don't want to learn how to be a chef. I don't have the time or desire to focus on it, considering my personal goals, so I let other people who are experts at cooking and have a strong nutritional knowledge base take care of making my food.

So, I guess *essentially* knowledge is about attraction. It's about building a relationship with learning. If you don't like what you're learning, learn something different.

The truth is that I believe gymnasts are the best athletes in the world. I've been training at it for years now, but I still can't do a fraction of what the good ones are able to do. The way they move and their ability to generate power from all kinds of different positions is simply amazing. It blows me away. Gymnasts can produce power from the most awkward positions. That's important in martial arts too, because no opponent is going to move you to a more comfortable position.

There's a kid who hangs around the gym whenever I go to train in gymnastics. He's shorter than I am, much thinner too, and he doesn't look powerful at all. Not even a little bit. But he makes me look weak. On my Facebook page I used to ask my fans to send me challenges. One day, one of my fans asked me if I could do a handstand push-up. That means leaning my knees on my elbows, with only my hands touching the ground, and pushing up. It requires power, strength and balance. Well, I couldn't do it. But this kid, this scrawny gymnast, he could do it, and more than one. I stopped counting at fifteen, I think.

In Case You Don't Have Time to Read...

... or don't *feel* like reading the whole book, at least remember this: pick a goal, make a realistic plan to reach that goal, work through each step of the plan, and repeat.

If it seems like a simple concept, that's because it *is* a simple concept. But it's not so easy to execute. The reason I'm sharing my intimate stories and thoughts in a book is so that I can hopefully help foster what Aristotle called "the greater good"—by helping readers to be better. After I beat Jon Fitch, I told him it was the best thing that could've happened to him. I humbly submitted that the only way to see the defeat was as an opportunity to get better. That putting the defeat in a proper context would give him the same opportunities I've been afforded.

Another powerful Aristotelean term I heard used by a good friend is *arete*. It's a Greek word with no real equivalent in any other language so far as I can tell, but basically *arete* is about looking into your own soul and not only discovering what it is that can make you great, but also identifying the *source* of that greatness and activating it every single day of your life. It's the well you draw from when there's no other resource. It's the absolute truth that sits in the deepest part of your soul.

I hope that within these pages you'll find some of the answers to your "inner" questions, but that's not the whole point. The key, actually, is to get you to ask yourself all kinds of questions to which nobody knows the answers. Nobody but you.

This isn't the only book out there that can help you become better at being who you were meant to be. But this one is my version, and I've decided to write it my way, which means that sometimes I'll be telling you about injury rehab, while at other times the story will draw from anecdotes from three key periods in my life—childhood, the journey to becoming a fighter, and being the most *authentic* champion I can be. Sometimes I'll take a few words to quote someone who inspires me. Other times I'll break down the material in lesson format, with key steps and examples. Some of the stories or quotes I'll share with you, I've carried with me for years; others I conjured with the help of friends and family quite literally while writing this book.

And I did not write it alone. There is a team behind this story—in fact there are many teams.

Something important for you to know is that I hire to my weaknesses. I've always looked to learn from experts who know more than I do. Kristof Midoux, John Danaher and Firas Zahabi are great examples of those who have helped me excel inside the octagon (and there are many more, including coaches and training partners). It's the same outside the octagon. My team of Canadian and U.S. agents make things happen for the business side of my career, negotiating contracts, helping me build my anti-bullying foundation and playing a key role in my life in all things not directly related to fighting. The point is that I choose people close to me to help me put my life in to context and determine the most useful points. They help me find the best way to tell this story. They've kept me honest, I think.

* * *

"L'homme libre est celui qui sait rêver, qui sait inventer sa propre vie." The free man knows how to dream and how to invent his

own life. The philosopher Martin Gray said that. The first part of Gray's quote I interpret as looking within yourself and imagining the greatest things you'll ever do. The second part of the quote—knowing how to *invent* life—I interpret as the practical side of the equation. It's about the plan you must develop to make the dream possible. It's the preparation and work that have to be done to make it come true. Because dreams don't get made overnight. I started karate when I was seven years old. It took almost two decades of constant practice and dedication to get a shot at the title. Twenty years! And to be perfectly honest with you, most of that time I had no real idea exactly where I was going. At first, I thought I was going to be a wrestler, like Hulk Hogan. "One day, when you were nine, I found you watching wrestling on television," my mother recalls. "You turned to me and said: 'One day there'll be a *bonhomme* Georges (a Georges figurine).' It really freaks me out when I think of that."

What isn't in Martin Gray's quote, though, is the journey. Because no two journeys are alike. Nobody can pretend to know the journey another person takes to achieve his dreams. There are billions of people on the earth, and every single path is different. Especially for those who are deliberately on the road to self-invention or *reinvention*. But we all have to rely on our feet and our eyes.

How I Structured This Book

The essence of the story is broken down into five major parts: Mother, Mentor, Master, Maven and Conscience. Each section is connected to the voice of someone who changed my life, who played a key role and helped me become who I am today.

Mother takes you into the world of my childhood and some of those early, shaping lessons. You'll hear from . . . my mother. *Mentor,* which should also be known as the Ground Book, is where everything begins, and the voice is Kristof Midoux's. *Master*—or what you might also call the Transition Book—represents growth and transition, and the voice belongs to the great thinker and Brazilian Jiu-Jitsu teacher John Danaher. *Maven,* the Standing Book, draws on the wise words of Firas Zahabi, my friend and head coach, and expresses how people use their knowledge and continue their progress through life, becoming better versions of themselves. *Conscience,* the only part of the book written after the Carlos Condit battle, delivers a completely different point of view on the person I've become, through the voice of my longtime friend and manager Rodolphe Beaulieu.

Ground. Transition. Standing. The flow represents how a mixed martial artist fights, learns, progresses and evolves. While we will delve into fighting techniques, there's more to winning battles than fists and feet.

BOOK I

MOTHER

Maman

One thing about Georges: he'll always tell you exactly what he thinks. He was cut from the same cloth as his dad and granddad. Both were hardworking and very, very direct. His granddad was nicknamed 'The Bionic One'—*Le Bionic.* Anyway, he's very opinionated and not afraid to face the truth, even though he's able to let other people's insults slide off him like water off a duck's back. In fact, you want to know the real Georges? He stays friends with his foes. *Le v'la ton Georges!* There's your real Georges.

—My Mother

I'm scared.

'm scared because I'm thinking of a moment that changed my life and altered who I am, and I can't get away from it. I realize that being scared is part of who I am. Fear is the genesis of most of the good things that have occurred in my life. Fear is the beginning of every success I've lived.

But it affects my perspective, both physical and logical. That's the way it works. It doesn't just change what happens inside of you, it also immediately impacts how you relate to the world all around you. How—or if—you remember. Because of fear, other information that seems totally basic and elementary—like what you were doing and why you were there—are gone. The present loses its power when pitted against fear.

Fear is magical and possesses all kinds of superpowers. All it takes is a few words or a flash of images to trigger its strength. And the moment you see or hear whatever it is that scared you, your life changes.

And yet, because I'm scared, details I don't usually notice are right there in my mind—I can see them and their shapes, I can sense them, and I feel like I could reach out and touch them. But not the whole picture; some things dissolve.

And *that's* what happened to me on the day my good friend Dr. Sébastien Simard called my mobile.

In fact, I'm sitting here trying to think of where I was when the phone rang, but I can't remember. I'd like to know what I was doing when I took the call, but that's not possible either. The memories attached to that moment are lost somewhere inside me, and I know it's because of the fear.

What I can recall—and the clarity of that recollection is odd, like a slow-motion dream—is that I was standing in a long hallway, alone. I see white walls and a hall and I'm walking down the middle of it toward who knows where. The phone rings and I know I have to answer because it's my surgeon. I stop, which is odd because usually I walk and talk. But here I stop, I look at the screen and see his name, I push the button and I put the phone to my ear. And this is when he tells me: "Georges, you have a torn ACL. Your knee ligament is fully torn. You need major surgery. You're not fighting for a long time."

Ever since I was nine years old I've known the unique feeling generated by fear. It makes me laugh now, but that's because I know better. It's because, without the bullies and the assholes and the jerks, I would never have become who I am today. I would never have been lucky enough to prove them wrong. I would be somebody different, and nobody can know who that person would or might have been. I just don't care about the possibilities because I can't change any of the things that have come before me. All I know for certain is the present.

I've also known for a long time that fear comes in two packages: good and bad.

Here's an example of good fear. When I was twelve years old, my buddies and I would gear up on winter days and plan these big street fights in our neighborhood. *All* the kids from my street or my neighborhood. We wore these big, thick winter coats, toques and gloves to protect ourselves from the minus-30 Celsius Canadian winters. We'd have these epic battles and beat each other in the snow until someone gave up. I was pretty good at that, but sometimes I ate my share of whoopings, especially from the older kids. We were trying to prove who was tough and I was really proud, so, many times, I got whooped. There were no head shots, just body blows. It was fun. I was scared, but I went anyway because I didn't want to be teased for being scared. It taught me to be humble. You learn to understand that others can be stronger than you.

I wasn't always the strong one. Fear *made* me. It's why I am in love with my own fear. Don't misunderstand me: I don't *like* fear, but I do love it, and there's a major difference there. Because of what my fear makes me do. Because of how my fear has made me who I am. Some of my fears are terrifying, paralyzing, and I won't talk to you about those. They take my sleep and my comfort away from me. So not here, not now. Because I'm not ready for that yet. I can't. I won't. I'm not a machine.

MOTHER: *My Georges came out two weeks late. He had lesions on his face, and soon after that he had scabs all over. There were five or six doctors checking on him all the time. We were really scared for him.*

The truth is that I didn't start as a winner. When I was a kid, I was just another reject. I started at the bottom. I think all winners do.

It was a physical thing, most probably. For some reason I don't know, I was addicted to licking my lips. I couldn't stop. I'd chew on the collar of my shirt, or I'd lick the rim of my lips. At home, walking to school in the classroom, in the schoolyard, I'd constantly be licking my lips, round and round and round. This wasn't good, especially for a kid who always had skin problems.

In fact, my mother told me that even before I left the hospital where I was born, I had all kinds of skin issues. I got better, of course, and I grew up all right and everything, but then when I was eight I had to have a major kidney operation—ever notice that big scar on my lower back?—and after the operation I started having psoriasis problems. Again, I got better, but for a while I wasn't very pretty to look at . . . and no matter what, I couldn't stop licking my lips.

Eventually, I developed a red rim of raw skin around my mouth. I must have looked like a diminutive clown, or something else, something ridiculous. To the other kids around me, I was different, weird, an easy target. It would be my first pass at the world of losing.

Even though I'd been studying karate since the age of seven, I realized when I was nine years old that life isn't like a movie. The bullies will win. When you're alone and there are three of them, and when they're twelve years old and you're a skinny, funny-looking nine-year-old, you're screwed. You can do all the karate in the world, you can fight back with everything you've got, but you will not beat them. I wasn't the Karate Kid, because that's fiction. Even though fiction is inspired by reality, fiction in commercial art often omits some very important, very *traumatizing* nuances.

It was tough being bullied where I grew up because everybody knows everybody. I come from St-Isidore, a village of about 2,000 people that's about thirty minutes outside of Montreal. I didn't have that many friends. I got close to one kid, an immigrant from Colombia who didn't speak French or English. We got on just fine, probably because we couldn't speak to each other at first. We used sign language, although I'm pretty sure he knew what was happening. He's always been a really smart guy. I'm glad he stuck by me, and that we're still friends today.

I'm the kind of person who can deal with insults, but what actually really makes me angry is when somebody picks on someone I care for. That *always* ticks me off. Sometimes when I got picked on, I got really scared and I ran. But other times I was being humiliated in front of everybody and didn't have a choice: I *had* to stand and fight. I confronted danger even if I knew I wasn't going to come out on top. My thinking was, *At least I'll get my shots in and they'll regret it and hopefully they won't try again.*

After school, at lunchtime, during recess—it happened pretty much anytime, anywhere. Playing dodgeball, they'd throw the ball in my face on purpose. They'd throw it at me when I was on the sideline, just because. I'd be walking off, and *pow!* Right in the kisser. They'd laugh more and I'd hurt more because it was unexpected.

I was always angered by my treatment, but I tried not to show it. I went through all the emotions, sometimes fear and avoidance, and other times maybe I was learning to be brave. I once fought because they spit on my friend and me. I went in alone, pretending I'd forgotten something, and I took a swing at one of them. They were surprised, especially when I connected. I got him good. I swung for another one, and that was the mistake. They teamed up and I really paid for it. But sometimes you just can't walk away.

The truth is that bullying has helped make me who I am. Without it, without those obstacles, I might not be where I am. The story would be different. Bullying was part of the world I grew up in, at a key period in my life, and I got through it. It was mine to face and I did.

Every single day was the same. I'd get up, walk to school past the same houses, along the same streets, by the same trees. My world was four kilometers square and everything I knew lived inside it. One day, I started losing my lunch money. Then I started losing my pants. I had these cool Adidas tearaway pants, the ones with the buttons that run along the side and you can pull off with a stiff yank, like the professional basketball players had on television. Every day, they'd yank them off me and laugh. And so I lost my dignity. In front of all the kids I went to school with. Right there in the schoolyard. Some of the kids looked on and laughed. Some pointed and whispered. Others, who were just as scared as I was, hid in the shadows. They probably thanked their lucky stars it was me getting picked on and not them. I don't blame them. Because I remember and understand how they must have felt. Luckily, I could take it. And yet, for some reason, I kept wearing those same pants to school.

One night, I came home from school and told my parents how I'd lost my lunch money to bullies. My dad got up from the kitchen table, walked me straight over to the one of the bullies' houses, told his parents about what he had done to me and demanded an apology and a promise that he never do it again. Not only did this tactic not work, but I was totally embarrassed, and so I never told my parents again about being bullied. My mother says that the next time she heard I'd been bullied as a kid was in a television interview a few years ago, when I was in my twenties.

The bullies kept at me for almost three years—until they found a bigger reject than I was, I guess. Or maybe they just got bored with me. I don't know why they started leaving me alone, and frankly I don't care. Maybe I was getting bigger and they knew I was on the verge of becoming a black belt.

Maybe the most important lesson I learned from my youth is that I don't ever want to make someone else feel the way these bullies did to me.

MOTHER: *I used to play records with subliminal messages for Georges when he was young. It was relaxing music to calm* *him down, and the messages were always positive, like "You are a loved child" or "You are a great person," things like that. It was important to me that he feel good about himself.*

When he was eight, he had a major kidney operation. That's when he started psoriasis. He had just started karate too. I remember he'd cry after losing at first, but I kept every single one of his karate evaluations and you can see where he started and where he got to today. It's incredible.

Some people learn to lose. Others lose and learn. The latter is a much better approach in my opinion because it focuses the mind on the positives and keeps your thoughts away from the negatives. One of my favorite Japanese proverbs is "Fall down seven times, stand up eight." This understanding extends to all things, by the way, but you only learn it by losing a few times.

Winning is love. I cried when I won my first title. It was the best moment of my career. It literally was a dream come true. Losing, however, is a step along a much longer life path. And the only way to ascend to new and greater heights is to lose. I have a special relationship with losing. It scares me to death, but that doesn't mean I can't find a way of using it to my benefit. Because losing changes me and turns me into a better man.

The first time I learned and understood what losing actually means, I was just eight years old. I was in grade school and I remember it like it was yesterday. I can see it in my mind's eye. I recall the details quite vividly because it's also the first recollection of pain in my life.

We were in the schoolyard during recess and a bunch of bigger, tougher kids were playing on the snowbanks. Trust me, there was lots of snow in St-Isidore during the winter. It's what we call a *real* winter. At my school, the plows would push the snow into these great mounds at the end of the yard. They were so high you couldn't see what was on the other side of them. But they sure were fun to play on. The schoolyard became a fortress of snow.

So throughout the winters, at lunchtime, we'd get out there, eight and sometimes ten kids, and play King of the Mountain. It's a simple game: everybody starts at the bottom, you race to be the first one to reach the top of the mountain, and then you do anything and everything possible to stay there, on top, being king.

We were all trying to be kings. The toughest primary-school kids who had something to prove, they were all there. *Les p'tits toughs,* I called them—the little toughs. There were no rules. You could do anything, as long as you stayed atop that mountain.

The kids on my block didn't play King of the Mountain— they were too little or nerdy—so I had no idea how it worked, but I was curious. At first, I just stayed in the distance, watching this game, trying to understand. One day, leaning against the wall on the other side of the yard, I decided it didn't look that tough and I decided to give it a try.

At the start I was pretty scared, but I was also pretty agile. So I was doing well at first, pushing a few people around and avoiding major shoves and pushes myself. I was strong enough, I thought, to maybe become king. But what I didn't realize is that, to the others, I was just the new guy, the rookie, the fresh meat. The others kids knew each other and how each played, strengths and weaknesses, tactics and all that. So when you were the new kid coming into the game, everybody noticed. It's like in football, when a veteran sees a new guy on the other side and tells one of his buddies, "Let him through once or twice so I can get a shot on him." At some point, especially in sport, someone's going to test you and see what you're made of. That's just the way it is.

One of the kids I'd pushed out of my way was getting frustrated—his name was Joel Cavanagh, and I'll never forget it. After a shove, he turned to me and asked, "Georges, do you want to fight?" I thought he just wanted to wrestle, something to have a bit of fun on the mountain. And so I barely had the word *yes* out of my mouth when he landed a straight right to my nose.

THWACK!!!

I fell and rolled down the side of the snow mountain, all the way to the ground. Somewhat dazed, I could tell from the snow on the ground that my nose was bleeding. I grabbed a handful of flakes and pressed it to my face for two reasons: to stop the bleeding, and to hide my shame! Joel was a nice kid, and we actually talked about what happened afterward. He was frustrated by my staying power and he took me by surprise. Every kid in the yard saw me get knocked down. But I learned something from it that I'll never forget. I may have lost that mountain, but I won a valuable lesson that day: the power of the unexpected. I've been using it ever since.

The worst punches are the ones you don't see coming. The ones that don't give your brain an instant to prepare you for the blow. The ones looking for a place to connect. Especially when the thrust—be it a fist, knee or foot—strikes your temple or your chin. Those are the strikes you don't immediately feel. You can't. Your body gives priority to all of the power exiting it. The powerful and instant displacement of human matter is so great that your knees buckle, then cease to function. All of you ceases to function. And you go down.

As for the top of the mountain, let's just say that I learned the best way not only to become but also to *stay* king is to keep my eyes up and my hands ready at all times.

MOTHER: *Georges had all this energy and we had to find new ways of punishing him. We couldn't make him sit down in the corner; it wasn't possible. So when he was bad, I'd send him to the monkey bars in the front yard. I told him to go dump his excess energy there.*

At two months, he was sleeping through the night. He was nine months old the first time he stood, and he took his first steps at thirteen months. The truth is that he preferred to walk on all fours, backward, and he was constantly bumping into people. I took him to an audition for the Cirque du Soleil once, but it wasn't for him. He said he'd never wear tights like the acrobats. Never. They were all sorts of professional or Olympic gymnasts at the audition too. He didn't fit in that day.

As he grew up, he became more and more active, and he was always on his tiptoes. He could disappear if you didn't keep your eye on him, and all it took was a few seconds. One day, he was in the yard, tomato planting with his dad. Georges was two and a half. Dad turned around for barely a moment, and poof! Georges was gone, vanished. We looked for him and somehow found him halfway down the street, near the corner, watching traffic. It was scary . . .

Georges was never able to sit still for even thirty seconds. He was always hyperactive. That's how it was for his first years.

The best thing I did for him when he was young is buy him a kids' encyclopedia about dinosaurs. He studied that book and learned it by heart. He fell in love with dinosaurs and their history and asked for more, and more, and more!

Many people wonder why I'm so interested in dinosaurs and their history. The reason is actually really simple: dinosaurs were the biggest, most physically powerful creatures that ever walked the face of the earth, yet now they're gone. They ruled the planet for more than 150 million years, but then they became extinct, they just disappeared, and it fascinates me. Ever since my mom bought me that encyclopedia about dinosaurs, I've been obsessed. How could these unbelievably powerful, fearsome creatures completely disappear?

But I'm also fascinated by cockroaches. Unlike the dinosaur, the cockroach is built for and exists for one single purpose: survival. It's the total opposite of a dinosaur. Cockroaches are survival machines. Scientists believe they can survive very high levels of radiation from a nuclear blast, and that's just the beginning of the story.

The cockroach is one giant nerve, fine-tuned to everything around it: the environment and all immediate sources of potential danger. It's adaptable to almost any situation it encounters, and that's what makes the cockroach so interesting. It's a mobile radar system designed to identify and avoid threats.

The cockroach doesn't waste a single thing; every part plays a role. It can run up to three miles per hour. It has faster reflexes than humans beings. It can live by eating paper or glue. It has two brains, including one in its behind. It has a set of teeth in its stomach to help it digest food. It can squeeze itself as thin as a dime. It can go about forty minutes under water on a single breath. It has been practicing survival for over 280 million years. A female can stay pregnant her whole life. Its heart doesn't need to move or beat. It rests for 75 percent of its existence. It lives in cracks and nooks—so, anywhere. It survives at minus-32 degrees Celsius, no problem. It has one giant nerve from head to tail, and the hairs on its back legs measure disturbances in the air. And finally, it can live for a full week without its head, until it dies—just because it can't drink water anymore. For humans, the cockroach is rather scary and intimidating, very suspicious and totally repulsive. It doesn't even have a pretty name: the cockroach. But it persists.

Dinosaurs were huge and powerful; they could not adapt and they died out. And so the big difference between dinosaurs and cockroaches is adaptability: one is able to adjust, while the other, apparently, couldn't. Dinosaurs didn't make adjustments, either because they didn't feel they needed to, or couldn't understand that they needed to. They were slowly but surely dying out as food became scarce and their environment changed around them—be it temperature or the arrival of mammals.

The same analogy applies to fighting, and probably any other sport. It's not always the strong that survive. It takes brains, guts, tolerance and forward thinking. We've seen this since the beginning of mixed martial arts.

Maybe the greatest MMA inspiration for me is Royce Gracie, who defeated Gerard Gordeau in UFC 1. Royce is not a big man. He's about six feet tall and weighs 185 pounds. Gordeau is taller (six foot five), bigger and physically stronger. In fact, for the final of the very first UFC, few people thought Royce could win. Everyone believed his brother Rickson was the better all-around fighter and better suited to MMA. But it was Royce who got chosen to represent the Gracie family style of fighting. And in the final, it didn't take Royce long to get Gordeau to the mat, trap him in a chokehold and tap him out.

This match, for me, showed a new way of fighting. It showed how a smaller, lighter man could beat anybody. It showed how MMA is more than a fight, it's a strategy sport. (Some people don't see it that way yet, but eventually, they should.)

Royce went on to defeat many opponents who were much larger than him, including the legendary sumo champion Akebono. Akebono is six foot eight and almost five hundred pounds, and the fight lasted barely more than two minutes. Akebono got on top of Royce, but in a poor position. Royce squirmed into a better position, slowly, methodically, until he finally got hold of one of Akebono's gigantic arms. He locked the wrist and Akebono submitted.

"I did everything my trainers told me not to do," Akebono said after the fight.

"What you saw tonight is exactly what I trained to do," said Royce. "I knew I had to bring Akebono to the ground, and I knew that the best way to do that was to let him come to me. It worked perfectly."

When he fought Royce Gracie in 2004, Akebono was the dinosaur that couldn't adapt despite his superior metrics across the board. He was three times the size of Gracie, after all, and likewise had become expert at a style of fighting. Gracie was the more fluid fighter, and he stuck with the plan and tweaked it as he went, seeking new opportunities as the fight evolved. I'm not saying Royce was a cockroach in a derogatory sense, of course—he's one of my heroes—but his approach and style were certainly based on constantly adapting to the threat in front of him. What got the great, big Akebono was a simple wrist lock.

In many ways, my approach also tries to mimic the cockroach's survival-based existence: I constantly have to invent new ways of defeating different and more lethal opponents. And I've had to become more efficient as I progress through my career. This is a critical point because, like the cockroach, I want to confuse my opponent before the battle even takes place. I want to psych him out before we fight so I can have the mental edge.

One of the jobs I had when I was starting out as a mixed martial artist was as a bouncer in a nightclub near Montreal.

Every single time I went to work, I had meatheads challenging me to a fight. It still happens nowadays, and it's always in clubs: guys come up to me, take one look at me and tell me they can kick my ass. I don't mind at all; it's all part of the game for me. What I used to do when guys got excited at the nightclub is say, "Hey, I can't hear what you're saying, let's go talk about this outside." They'd immediately think we'd be about to fight, so they'd eagerly follow me out. Once we'd get outside the club, I'd tell them they weren't allowed back in because they were acting like jerks, and they'd be welcome another day, when they were calmer (and sober). It pissed a lot of them off, but that's all right. It happens. These were just harmless drunks trying to show off their physical strength, and the best technique was to outsmart them; psych them out—avoid it altogether.

There are still many, many fighters who focus on their brute strength before perfecting their technique. But they often run into a wall as they fight better, smarter opponents. In sports, we see the David-versus-Goliath example all the time.

I've never been the biggest guy in the octagon, and I don't ever want to be either. My goal is to be the most efficient, quickest-thinking fighter. I aim to be flexible, open-minded and ready for any situation. And so, I may love the dinosaurs and their stories, but I'm inspired by the cockroach: the ultimate adapter and the greatest survivor.

MOTHER: *What I remember best is that whenever Georges started something, he never stopped. He'd see something on TV, and then he'd go alone somewhere and practice it until he got it. Only then would he come back and show you what he could do. When he was ten, he saw people on TV walking on their hands, and so he decided he was going to do the same. He spent two whole years walking on his*

hands at home. I'd call the family in for dinner and you'd
see these two little legs bobbing in behind the kitchen table.
That was my Georges.

My father first introduced me to Kyokushin karate when I was seven years old. He had practiced karate for years and was a black belt himself, and so he taught me the basic principles and movements in the basement of our home, which hasn't changed much since my childhood. When you walk down there you can see the punching bags and gloves and all the other equipment I've gathered over the years.

When my dad was content that I had learned the basics, he registered me at a local karate school. I remember my very first class, a brand new white belt holding my brand new *gi* taut against my body. There had to be a hundred other kids in that class—and, in the ensuing weeks and months, I lost fights to most of them.

After a while, my peers and I had the opportunity to graduate to green belt, but during the examination, I looked around and noticed we weren't a hundred anymore. Now we were about fifty. As the years passed by, the number continued to dwindle, and I noticed that the fewer the number of regular students, the more fights I won. I was still losing a lot, mind you, but I kept going forward. And I believed my instructors, who constantly reminded me that I would keep getting better, that I had superior athletic skills, that I was making progress.

I also listened to my dad, who told me I should never quit, no matter how slowly it seemed I was developing or how long it took me to improve. One of my friends even remarked that I was "stubborn," "independent"—"hyperactive," even! Years later I can confirm that he was on the mark: once, to prove a point, I walked on my hands for almost two years.

By the time I got to the brown belt level, we were fewer than ten students, and when I was almost thirteen years old and going for my first black belt, there were only two of us standing there. This is when I first reflected on the recent past and realized that, though I had lost a lot more fights than I had won during the previous five years, I had changed: *now, I was finding new, innovative ways of losing fights.* I was learning from my losses, and this led to me win some close fights that I used to lose before.

With the help of my father and my teachers, I learned about resiliency, but at thirteen, I wasn't yet approaching losing from a philosophical perspective. At one point I had even tried to quit karate altogether. I was twelve years old and tired of losing and tired of my teacher, who, in retrospect, was a great mentor but a hard man. We used to get slapped around and barked at a lot. In fact, in today's world, he probably wouldn't be allowed to be as tough on kids as he had been, but this was another time, another era. One day I told my dad I was quitting karate for good. He wouldn't hear of it. He just looked up at me and stared into my eyes: "You can quit when you're a black belt," he stated plainly. "Don't ever quit anything until you've reached the end." He went back to whatever he was reading, which was the indicator that that was the end of the conversation. I had no choice but to go back. Thank goodness I did.

Funnily, one of my sisters was in the same class and she too decided to quit. But instead of talking about it with my dad, she hid in the cornfields behind our house so that nobody would force her to go back. We still laugh about that one. I'm thankful to my dad, though, because this was one potentially lost opportunity that would have altered my life for the worse. He turned this seemingly small episode into an eternal truth: always finish what you've started.

Of course, I never actually *liked* losing, and I still had no idea how losing would help make me a better person. Between the ages of thirteen and seventeen, I was living according to a new emotion: anger. I didn't understand why I'd been bullied, and it really bothered me. I wondered what I'd done wrong, and what was wrong with me. I decided I wasn't going to relive my past as a bullied kid, and at first, as I kept getting better at karate, I just wanted to learn more ways of breaking arms and hurting people. I had a lot of hatred, a lot of anger. And I really wanted revenge on the bullies.

That's what happens after you've been bullied. Some bullied kids become class clowns because they want to be liked so badly that they think making people laugh will bring them back to respectability. I know people like that. Other bullied kids go into hiding and aim for invisibility, hoping the world never again takes notice of them. Some bullied kids become bullies themselves—not because they enjoy being bullies, but more because they figure that if they do, nobody else will bully them anymore.

And some choose to fight the world of bullies on their own.

MOTHER: *Georges never opened his school books a lot, but he always made sure to do the necessary work and pass all his courses. He also always respected his teachers and elders.*

Although I wasn't the type who was going to step out and start fights, I decided I wasn't going to walk away from one ever again. This kind if thinking translated to how I behaved in class with other students.

One of the important lessons I learned from my parents is always to respect authority figures like teachers. While some of our teachers were pretty annoying and rude, one of them was really warm and kind. She always encouraged me and treated me like I had something special. Of course, she taught religion and spirituality. I decided I was going to police her course and keep the kids under control so she could teach uninterrupted. This isn't a bad thing, but it certainly didn't make me any more popular at school.

One day, this guy kept on teasing me, and I decided I'd had enough. We got into a fight, and not only did I win, but I broke his arm.

And then my world changed.

After thinking about what I'd done, I was a little ashamed of having hurt him so bad, and I thought people wouldn't want to be near me. I actually thought I'd be cast out even further from the norm. But it was just the opposite. Now I was popular. I had been a reject for a long time, and then one day I got in a fight and broke a guy's arm and all of a sudden I was popular.

I knew it was bullshit. It pissed me off that I'd become popular because I'd kicked a guy's ass. I thought it was stupid, even though people "liked" me now. I thought people were stupid, and I didn't give a crap what they thought of me anymore, not at all, and I didn't hesitate to tell them exactly what I thought of them.

MOTHER: *By the time he got to high school, I think he was very lonely. He was home a lot. He didn't have many friends, but I remember our dogs wanted to sleep next to his bed or in front of his door. He had a special relationship with those dogs, a shepherd and a collie. They followed him everywhere.*

I think the reason he was so lonely is that he didn't know what to do with his genius—"son génie," as we say in Quebec. I felt he was purposely isolating himself from others. He did have two very nice girlfriends for a while, but I think they became possessive, and you never tell Georges what to do. His training always comes first. Always.

I rejected the world I'd come from. I lost my bearings, my foundation. I could feel the world shifting beneath my feet, and my struggle was to keep balance. It was ridiculous that people would start respecting me now because of this event. So I realized it wasn't real respect, it was fear, and that pissed me off even more! So I focused on training because it was the only thing I was sure I wanted to be doing. I withdrew, slowly, surely, into my own shell. I went back to my dad's basement and the gym. It was the only thing that made me feel good. Back when I was a kid going through this for the first time, I didn't know what else to do. I didn't know what I was going to do with my life. I had no idea what I would become. It just felt good to be training. Working. Moving forward.

So I slowly drew away into my own world, my own invented existence.

MOTHER: *I have to admit that at first we didn't understand the Georges we saw fighting in the octagon. We didn't know where the anger or the vengeance came from. This inner rage was foreign to us. For his first-ever fight in Laval, he had to convince me to go, and he kept talking about the technical side of martial arts. He said to me, "Tell me what you think after you see me fight, not before."*

We haven't missed any of his fights since.

He's changed a lot too, like he's transformed himself. How he speaks, the way he moves, the style he dresses. He's always still the same Georges, but when I see him on TV, I see that he's created another personality.

It makes me wonder sometimes where he comes from.

A lot of people who have known me for many years say there are two Georges. They see and hear two of me, they say. There is one Georges they've always known. And then there is this other Georges who, if not entirely different, seems unknown and surprisingly distinct.

My mother often says she doesn't recognize me when she hears me giving media interviews. My own entourage, who spend more time with me than anyone ever has—sometimes they just look at me after I've spoken, and they stare. Like they weren't expecting those words to come out of me. Like it's not really me.

I think I know when I first noticed the change—the *other* Georges, as they call it. I was nineteen years old and had just started my MMA career. The years before turning nineteen had been long and tough and filled with doubt. Darkness. The dreams I had were still stuck inside me, and I didn't know how to voice them yet. I started behaving differently, making decisions that surprised some people. Like going to New York City to seek out new coaches, new knowledge.

I understand what people mean by their idea of two Georges. There's me in a hostile environment, when I need to be hard and without pity, and then there's me when I'm in relaxed surroundings. There's quite a difference . . .

At the end of high school, I stopped talking to people, stopped connecting and just focused on myself. I discovered a darker side, a darker place in my existence. I'm not sure exactly how to explain it. I just think it was part of my evolution. I've been a good and nice person at times, and it has helped me win opportunities, and other times I've been pitiless because that's what the situation demanded of me. Genetics and environment are the determining factors in that equation. Where I come from, and the people who came before me, helped make me who I am today.

Determinism is something I strongly believe in. I have the

illusion that I control all of my actions, but in reality I don't. It's like a pool table—you hit the cue ball and it strikes the other balls and sends them on a path that's beyond your control, even if you know where the balls are going. Life is like that, just more complex. It's the butterfly effect, and each gesture has an impact on the final result. It means I control most of my reactions, and as I get better and acquire more knowledge, my preparation to meet my fate is improved.

The key has always been simple, though: discovery. Even though other people had started voicing their opinions on my potential, I remained silent. Until I discovered exactly what it is that I wanted to do: become a mixed martial artist. That discovery gave belief to my inner dreams because I started seeing the concrete possibility that I could become a fighter, a true fighter. And so the change was going from having visions about my life to living them concretely.

At this stage in my life I left many, many things behind. I constantly heard Kristof's words whispered in my ear, and it triggered a reaction inside me and I realized: this is what I want to do. I want to become champion of the world in mixed martial arts.

And then, all of my energy, everything I had inside of me, went toward achieving that unique goal. I wasn't making sacrifices anymore, I was making *decisions*. Train instead of party. Work instead of play. Perfect practice instead of casual repetition.

I started living life with purpose and direction. In the words of Buddha: "First, intention; then, enlightenment."

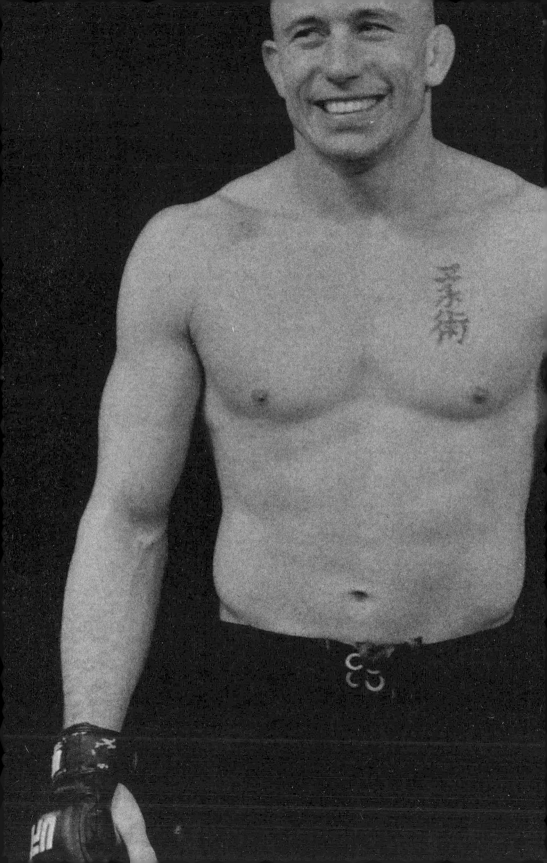

BOOK 2

MENTOR

The Ground Book

WITH
KRISTOF MIDOUX, SENSEI

I was only fooling myself.

I still wasn't on top of fear, even if I might have thought I was. Being in the *now,* at this moment, having just heard that surgeons would be cutting into my knee, became a bad idea. This was not a good thing for me, fighting my fear in the *now.* I took some hard shots and the fear took me down, but I thought I'd be able to reset my mind after a while. Get my feet back underneath me. But I was wrong, and I panicked.

The *now* is usually when the fear tricks you, when you think you're okay again. It gets you to think there's an easy solution, a simple fix. That's what happened to me: I decided I'd fix my torn ACL right *now.*

I went from fear of never fighting again to wanting to be able to fight next week. The fear got me thinking that I needed to fix the problem in the next twenty-four hours, right away, as soon as possible—NOW, RIGHT FUCKING NOW! I rushed home and sat on the computer and started looking up surgeons. I Googled it: surgeons, anterior cruciate ligament, ACL, best in the world. I made a list of names, people I'd never heard of. I called around to my team and told them the news, but that I didn't want them to worry and I had a plan. I wanted to do things quickly. I spoke with Firas and asked him to help with my search of surgeons, that I could go in tomorrow and get my knee opened and fixed. Because the fear convinced me I was ready, I could do this, and the earlier the better. The fear took control because that's what it's supposed to do, and I should have known that. I should have remembered. Instead, I freaked out.

Fear hates logic, and it puts blinders next to your eyes and thoughts and forces you to focus on one single thing—as long as that one thing isn't the fear itself. This is not good.

Don't get me wrong: fear can be a good thing, and there's no way you can eliminate it from your life. In fact, eliminating fear from your life is a lie, or it's a mental illness. That's it, nothing more. Anyone who says they don't feel fear is a liar. Guys who say they don't feel fear are full of shit or they're plain crazy. Major denial issues.

I remember hearing a story about soldiers going into battle and showing no fear, and the guy said it was really simple (I'm paraphrasing here): "There are two kinds of men: those who want to go out and fight—the crazy ones—and the ones who are afraid to go, but they go anyway. They're the courageous ones." I realized at this moment that it takes fear to make a person courageous. And I like that, because courage says something about you.

The result is that, after a while, you get practice at being courageous. You understand how to move forward against fear, how to react in certain situations. You just get better. It doesn't mean you stop feeling fear—that would be careless—but it means you have earned the right to feel confidence in the battle against fear.

MENTOR: *It's in training that you see the real Georges and see how dangerous he really is, like an assassin. In fact, I think he's too nice to his training partners. You can see it in their faces and hear them after sparring: "I did this to Georges" or "I passed his guard and it was easy." They don't realize that*

Georges is doing that on purpose to put himself in harder sit-
uations. But that, too, is part of concealment: letting people
imagine your weaknesses and question your strengths. But
these people who train with Georges never really get a chance
to be in a real fight with him, and they shouldn't want to.

Many people call him the French Hurricane. His ability to pop up at any time, to overtake center stage and to submit men with his awe-inspiring force, is legendary. Kristof Midoux, after all, once knocked out an opponent in nine seconds. I think it's an MMA record, and it came in his first professional fight. He stepped into the ring, the referee started the bout, Kristof moved forward and, with a single flying knee, knocked his opponent out cold. Everyone in the room felt a surge of power, like seeing a comic book hero absorb his opponent and all he has ever owned. One swallow, and a person disappeared.

Other people call Kristof Midoux *"le phénix,"* the phoenix, the mythical bird that burns into ashes as it darts across the sky. Maybe, to some people, he really is a fiery ball of power that blazes down from above. Maybe he is the ashes that give rise to the self. Or maybe, like the classic story of the phoenix, he signals immortality.

Whatever you choose to call him, let me tell you this: Kristof Midoux is the single most important figure in my becoming a mixed martial artist, and the only reason why I understood so many years ago that I could become a champion.

When I was barely sixteen years old, I had no idea what I was going to do with my future. I was becoming a loner at high school. All I wanted to do was go to Kahnawake, the Mohawk reserve near Montreal, to watch local MMA events when my mother let me. There were times when I wasn't allowed to go— not because of the violence, necessarily, but because some adult magazine sponsored the event. The sport was fresh and new and I felt a special connection to what I could see happening inside the octagon. The king inside that octagon during those years was Kristof Midoux.

Midoux was larger than life for me, and at six foot two, 240 pounds, he stood for pure, unstoppable power. He's European, and despite his French citizenship, he'd chosen to fight out of St-Joseph-de-Sorel, Quebec. He had the same Kyokushin karate background as I had, and on top of this, he owned and ran an MMA gym in downtown Montreal.

> **MENTOR:** *Canada accepted me when I was young, and had been very good to me. I felt really good here—this is where my life in sport took off—so I thought I should be good to this country. France has never accepted my sport—not yet, anyway—so I've never represented France or carried its colors, and I don't think I ever will. Even at the world competitions, it's the Canadian anthem that I'd play, and my sponsors come from Russia.*

After seeing him fight, I decided I would track him down and find a way to become his pupil.

> **MENTOR:** *Some people at the reserve had said this kid was talking about me and wanted to meet with me. I didn't pay much attention to it, but eventually I'd have to . . .*
>
> *I was wandering down the sidewalk one day, running errands, and I saw this car stop half in the middle of the road. It got my attention. Suddenly, I saw this kid with short blond hair come out of it and run toward me. He literally chased me down the sidewalk.*

I was driving up St-Laurent Boulevard in the heart of downtown Montreal when I saw Kristof walking down the sidewalk. Immediately, I became excited, knowing this was the opportunity to speak with him alone. I half pulled over in my car and slammed on the brakes, leaving the vehicle and blocking a lane on St-Laurent. I ran out from the driver's side and sprinted over to Kristof. He stopped and looked me up and down curiously. He smiled and said *bonjour.* I responded by telling him I'd been looking for him because I badly wanted him to me my teacher.

MENTOR: *He had these piercing blue eyes and this short blond hair, he looked everything like a sixteen-year-old boy. "Kristof! Kristof! You're the champion of the Indian reserve!" he said. "I do karate just like you. I want to become strong like you in this sport. What do I need to do?"*

"Why me?" Kristof asked.

"Because I've seen you fight, and we both come from the same background, and I believe you can teach me many things," I responded.

MENTOR: *Looking into his face and seeing the way he was determined, the way he addressed me, I just had a feeling in my gut, a good feeling I couldn't resist. So I invited him to "come tomorrow" to my gym in downtown Montreal and to train with my fighters and me. I said I'd take a look at him and see if and how I could help him.*

"There's a problem, though—I don't have any money."

"That's okay," he replied. "Neither do I."

MENTOR: *When he came back after our first meeting, I saw immediately that there was something to do with this kid. That's why I couldn't leave him behind. I told him that if he'd stay disciplined and come regularly to train, I'd help him out.*

I saw from the very first day that he loved training, he lived and fed off of it, and nothing would tire him. Nothing. That's also why I wanted to help him. I did everything I could to exhaust him, to make him fall from fatigue, to break his will and his resolve, but he just kept coming back to me. He kept coming for more, day after day. It was like a battle between us in many ways to see who could outlast the other. Every time he came to train—he'd go two solid hours, take a little ten-minute break and then start going again—I saw more and more potential.

My life literally changed when I met Kristof.

It started at the first moment on the first day that I stepped into Kristof's gym. He looked at me, stared straight into my eyes, pointed at me and said, *"I'm going to make a champion out of you."* It really scared me. Not only was Midoux a legend where I came from, but he looked every bit the part of a professional MMA fighter: bruised, tattooed, cut from a rock. And he had the intense disposition to match.

In my head, I thought it would be possible to become a champion, but I never expressed it to anybody. I thought maybe it was just another daydream, a mental trick, another fantasy that existed inside my head alone. But Kristof believed in me.

MENTOR: *He had a crazy life: no money, a few shitty part-time jobs—including one as a garbageman—a crap car filled with more crap, but he never complained. After a tough workout,* *we'd get a quart of milk, two small pieces of crappy chicken or a cheap salad, and despite this cheap, shitty food, he'd look up at me and say he felt strong, that he was ready to go. He was always ready to go, and he hasn't really changed much when it comes to this.*

The only solace I found during this time was from training and fighting in the gym, and Kristof encouraged me to stick to that. Kristof, in the meantime, did what he was good at: getting me mentally ready for the challenges that lay ahead. A lot of people expressed doubts about Kristof and alluded to his questionable reputation, but I just didn't listen to them. He was different from anyone I'd ever met, and his interests were my interests, so I went with what I knew and felt was right.

As we started training together, he did something very interesting.

MENTOR: *I made Georges realize his own power by giving him choices. We'd be in my gym, for example, and I'd invite fighters who were already professional and on television.*

He made me fight against all the "regional" guys who were competing regularly on the circuit. Guys I'd see on television destroying everybody. And he made me face them. We'd get to the gym for training, I wouldn't know the plan for the day, and he'd just toss me in the ring.

MENTOR: *Then I'd ask Georges: "Between these two guys, which one do you think is strongest?"*
In those days, you had local legends like David Loiseau and Jason St-Louis. St-Louis, especially, was seen as an assassin in those days. But I knew how those guys were

fighting, St-Louis and Loiseau. I knew their thinking. When you're a professional, you get a feeling just from touching someone or being close to them. You sense an aura of strength, of power, of danger—or you don't. Some guys will be standing ten meters from you, but even at that distance you can sense them, and you feel a certain power. I wanted to teach this to Georges and just let him feel how strong he is, so I had to show him his strength by using other fighters' strengths, and by putting obstacles in his way.

I used those reputed assassins like victims, really, but they had no idea what I was doing. In fact, I had to draw them out to our gym and trick them into training with us. I'd say, "Hey, come on over for a free seminar and free training sessions." They'd walk in and see Georges's nice blue eyes and his pretty blond hair . . . fresh meat. They'd have no idea what power he had in him. Georges didn't know what he was doing there either. He was scared and intimidated.

At first, I refused to fight; I was too scared. They were really strong and powerful and I didn't think I could beat them. But Kristof's voice was a constant whisper in my ear, telling me, reminding me and cajoling me into believing I was better than everyone. He'd lean in close to me, put his powerful hand on my shoulder or grip my forearm, and say: "You're better. You're strong, very powerful. You can defeat this opponent. Believe me, and believe in yourself." Eventually, I took the step, I crossed the line, and it was the best thing I ever did. At seventeen years old, true to his promise, I really dominated those fighters. That's how I found my own source of belief and transitioned into the world of MMA as a fighter.

This became Kristof's trademark. He kept putting me in

situations where I didn't think I could win, but he always knew I would.

> **MENTOR:** *In terms of martial arts, I was brought up by the Japanese. Their "way" is part of who I am. I started when I was four years old. I've made people win battles they should have lost, and I've made others lose battles they should have won. It comes down to mental games, and knowing the difference between fiction and reality. The only true challenge I faced with Georges was his confidence. I had to find a way to help him believe in his own power.*
>
> *Georges is first and foremost a theorist. This is why I believe that one day he'll be a great teacher. It's also why I was able to put him in situations that everyone else would have failed in. He has a superior intellect, especially when it comes to the martial arts. So I designed lessons made for him.*

I love learning and discussing ideas and the way people have thought throughout the history of mankind. I'm drawn to traditional philosophy and philosophers—in a completely informal way. The school of thought or the historical relevance make no difference to me. What matters to me is the practical application of the novel thinking. This doesn't mean I'm an expert who can teach a class about philosophy; it means I have found a way to incorporate traditional philosophy into my way of life to help make it better. It means that a certain kind of knowledge enhances my life. That's why I post an inspirational quote on my Facebook page every week. I choose one that I think helps me be a better person, and I share it with my fans.

> **MENTOR:** *The difference between Georges and everyone else I saw in training was his discipline. There have been a lot of*

people in Canada who have practiced this sport, kids who are strong but don't have what it takes to go far. Georges—you see right away that martial arts is part of who he is, the discipline, the understanding. Even that first day, if you bothered to open your eyes you could see he'd go far. He was totally pure: no smoking, no drinking, absolute focus—he was obsessed by the sport. I could see it in his eyes.

Now, you can't let an idiot believe he's strong—it won't work and he will fail. But Georges was extremely strong and had amazing capacities and potential, but he didn't know how to believe in himself. He'd see others do well, and he never wanted to lack respect for anyone else.

The first time I saw St-Louis, I didn't want to go out there on the mat, but Kristof told me it was too late—he was waiting for me, and there I was. I *had* to go out there. He didn't leave me any choice. He'd scream at me, "Go get changed now!" He turned to St-Louis and said, "Here's a new kid, don't be too hard on him." But then he'd turn to me and give me *my* instructions: "Take the initiative, jump them, and beat them as fast as possible."

MENTOR: *I knew I had to let him see how much stronger than everyone else he always was. That was the hardest part of my job—to let him see his own potential. I forced and imposed my will on him. I played tricks on him to test him, and he passed every time. Everything I asked, everything I instructed, everything I said to do, Georges did. When I made him believe that professionals train five to six hours a day, he believed me.*

And then it happened. I started taking guys down five, six times in a row. At the end of some of our fights, there'd be holes in the walls. It was total chaos. Bodies would fly all over the place. But it was over, and somehow I had won. Baffled, they'd turn and ask, "Who the hell is that kid?" Like in a cartoon strip.

The thing I had to learn, and I keep learning this lesson in my life every day, is how to take the fear's power and use it to become better. But fear is smart, and many times it's smarter than you and it makes you do stupid, irrational things, or it makes you forget simple things—like where you were standing the moment your life changed in major way. Because changes do happen from moment to moment.

The key, I discovered, is to understand fear and how it works. What I want to do is demystify fear. I don't have a choice, because fear walks next to you everywhere in life. It has a reason for being there. People feel fear because they sense a threat. Sometimes it comes from physical pain: something unseen falls on your head, it hurts, and you're immediately scared. That's normal, and what the fear is doing is telling you to be careful, to get out of the way because it doesn't want *something else* to fall on your head. So fear's purpose is ultimately good—that's what people forget. Fear is designed to bring you to a safe place. In this case it's telling you to get the hell out of the way. Simple human logic.

The problem with fear is that it's talking to you about the future—it says, *MOVE! Something else that is bad and painful could be coming your way and might fall on your head.* And people are like animals in this instance; they tend to follow their instincts. They follow the fear and dedicate all their energy to moving out of the way, toward safety. They brace and tense because of fear, and this creates a surge of adrenaline.

Often, the bad side of fear is the adrenaline, or more precisely, the side effects of adrenaline. When you feel fear, your hormones go nuts. Essentially, your muscles get fed with rocket fuel, your metabolic rate goes through the roof (your heart starts pumping hard) and your blood sugar levels follow. Your awareness changes, meaning all of your focus is controlled by the fear. It's trying to protect you, wondering if something else is about to fall on your head (which is why I think there are things that I remember and other things that I don't). Simply put, fear makes you instantly ready for a fight, no matter where you are.

Once fear enters your life—whether it's been there for a second or a lifetime makes no difference—it will take you in one of two directions: empowerment or panic. That's where the expression "like a deer in headlights" comes from. The deer is panicking and the panic—the extreme expression of fear—makes him stand there, unable to act. This marks the end of the deer, usually, and it's not a happy end. Don't be a deer. Dumb deer die a depressing death.

We have to start by remembering that fear is there to help steer us away from risk. It's supposed to help us get better. But the way fear helps us is by turning us into very powerful machines— it sends adrenaline throughout our bodies and makes us all-powerful super-beings capable of lifting cars or carrying people out of a burning building. Think about firemen—with training, these brave people learn how to harness their adrenaline so they can walk into the inferno, do their jobs and save lives.

This is what happened early on in my career in my very first fight in the UFC, against Karo Parisyan. The truth is that I wasn't considered much of a contender when I came up as a professional. I was supposed to be the mincemeat for upcoming stars like Parisyan. I understood and accepted my role, but that doesn't mean I wasn't going to go for it.

In that fight against Parisyan, I got caught in his kimura on two separate occasions. The first time, he had me, but the hold wasn't secure and I quickly got out of it. The second time was actually really bad. The commentator was going nuts too, I could hear him screaming, "Kimura!" and everybody in my corner—me included—thought I was done for.

Very few people understand how I got out of his kimura the second time, but I knew my own truth, my life situation: I had nothing. I had to win, I just *had* to, and couldn't accept anything else. If I didn't win, I couldn't live to the end of the month. I had to pay rent, buy food. I was ready to die to get out of that hold. *Break my arm if you have to,* I thought. I didn't have a choice. So I used the surge of adrenaline to roll him, got him on his back and won. The fear-based adrenaline, the training and the empowerment of making a decision all helped me to victory.

Of course, I didn't know all that at the time, but it wasn't just instinct kicking in. Before some of my fights I've had what are called adrenaline dumps. This is a fancy way of saying that fear is trying to take possession of my body. Adrenaline dumps suck, and in my case, when I get one, I can't feel my legs. It was so invasive and disturbing once, when it happened right before entering the octagon, that I had to ask Rodolphe to slap and shake my thighs because I couldn't feel them anymore. The look of mixed horror and surprise on Rodolphe's face said it all. This doesn't happen so often anymore, but that's because I got used to harnessing that adrenaline and turning it into power I save for the octagon.

That's where the real secret lies: learning how to use the power of fear. But the solution really does lie with the beholder. If a person is unsure about who he is and what his life goals are, the fear takes over his body and does what it wants with it.

Fear freezes your actions because it takes you into the world of what-if, and that's the worst place anybody can be. This is when you start doing stupid things like predicting the future, or thinking your career as a mixed martial arts world champion is going to end suddenly. Forecasting doom and gloom is not only useless, but detrimental. It's giving away all your power to fear and letting it take over your life. The consequences stink. Once you start doubting yourself, you're vulnerable. That's when critics' words start to influence your thoughts. *Maybe he can knock me out,* you think. *Maybe I'm not that strong. Maybe he will catch me and put me down.* Someone says about you, "He doesn't have a chin," and you think it's true. It gets inside your head, like a smell you can't scrub away. *Maybe I don't have a chin for real.*

And then one day you get tired of it, of the self-doubt, of the constant questions, of the disbelief. And you get angry at them—at *yourself.* And you realize it's time to rebel. To fight. Because it's from fighting—from *doing*—that you get your confidence back. Getting back in the ring and performing, doing well.

If it sounds like I'm talking about myself, that's because those were the thoughts that went through my mind after losing to Matt Serra.

Over time, if you don't learn to deal with your fear, your body won't like it. This is when you discover the meaning of the word *stress,* which leads to all kinds of nasty stuff like colds, infections, various and mysterious kinds of weird aches and pains all over your body, constant fatigue, inability to eat, and, for some very unfortunate people, sexual disorders.

* * *

I have a secret for not letting fear spiral out of control. It doesn't always pop up in my mind right away, but I'm getting better at it. That's the key, really, for any change in life: Do you get better at it, or worse? I think it's important to have a list of reminders to fight fear the right way—and that means getting away from the place fear is taking you. The what-if world of fear makes you project bad things into the future—*your* future—and we know this is useless.

This is something I've discussed many times with Firas, my coach. Whenever I get into a situation where I'm letting fear take over my life, I try to remind myself of his line, "Georges, don't star in your own movie."

Many people feel this kind of fear when they get on planes, for example, but it's totally illogical. You don't freak out when you get into your car for a drive, so why freak out when you sit in a much safer plane? Just ask Bruce Willis . . .

If you look at fear from an emotional perspective, it will drag you down into panic. But if you can look at it objectively, analytically, only then can you make it work for you. When you master this, you open new avenues to generate power and knowledge. You discover new ways of thinking. You learn that fear can be a natural ally, a homemade power source.

If you find ways of staying in the present, fear can only help you. It's all about preparation. Every Saturday afternoon that I'm in Montreal, I go to Tristar Gym and train with fellow professional fighters. I want to fight guys who are better than me in all kinds of techniques. I want my training to be harder than my actual fights so I can be prepared to face the toughest opponents—so I can be ready to deal with fear.

If you prepare your subconscious for highly stressful situations, you can create harmony with your fears. You can tame fear like a wild animal and use it to your advantage. To achieve this, though, you have to be fully aware of your own intentions and have an honest understanding of the goals you're pursuing and how they relate to the individual life you're inventing.

So the key is coming back into the present, and there are all kinds of easy ways of achieving this. The first is just to take a look around and remind yourself of where you are right now, and how everything is okay in this place. This doesn't mean there aren't concerns about the future—I knew, for example, that I'd need surgery at some point—but it wasn't the key thing right at that moment. Right at that moment the key was to take a deep breath. If you've ever really watched me during a fight, one of the most important things I do in between rounds is breathe deeply and slowly so I can relax, I have been told. People who meditate believe that four deep breaths—in through the nose, fill the belly, exhale slowly through the mouth—are proven to relax you. I agree. Try it, and you'll feel it in the middle of your chest, the thorax.

Zen Buddhists, when they meditate, have a way of always staying connected to the present, no matter where their thoughts take them. They ring what's called a mindfulness bell. So they sit and breathe and meditate and, when the bell rings, they open their eyes and reconnect with where they are so that they stay attached to the present. They are thankful for being there, and often you'll see them smile while they meditate. I like that.

At one point a few years ago, I went through a tough situation with a girl. I cared for her deeply, but we constantly quarreled. The last thing I hoped for was to create hurt, but change was necessary. Yet it seemed like the thought of her was stuck to the inside of my head. When I closed my eyes, I couldn't escape her. And when I opened them, she seemed to appear everywhere I looked. This only made the situation worse, and I truly felt at a loss, unable to make any final decision.

A friend of mine, seeing the effect the situation was having on me, gave me some very good advice. He said, "Do what the Buddhists do. Do nothing."

It didn't give me the right answer, it didn't show me the right path or reveal any great truth lurking somewhere. It just gave me a break, and I needed a break. It gave me a chance to think about something else. It told my brain, my network, that I wasn't going to think about her or our problems for a while, and that was okay. It let me focus on other things and turn my attention to my training, for example, or just having fun with my buddies.

I think that the Buddhists have a great approach to their lives: they sit and reflect and try to always stay connected to the present. This is how they learn to accept what the world has to offer, no matter the situation. This is how they achieve happiness—by never aiming for it directly.

The key lesson here, to me, is that sometimes you don't need to decide right then and there what's going to happen. You need to understand that the world keeps turning and nobody needs to rush into any harsh decision or situation. It's okay to do nothing sometimes.

A few weeks later, I ran into the same friend and we went for a bite at a great Portuguese chicken place in North Montreal. He asked me how my heart was feeling now that I had spent some time "doing nothing." Even though I hadn't found a final resolution to the problem, I told him that I felt much better about everything. I asked him how long this could go on, and he said that some Buddhist monks spend their whole lives "doing nothing."

Then he quoted John F. Kennedy: "There are risks and costs to a program of action, but they are far outweighed by the long-term risks and costs of comfortable inaction." In other words, doing nothing is fine for a while, but the goal isn't to avoid the issue. (Zen Buddhists would likely disagree with me on this point.) The goal is to reflect calmly about all the facts, and to make a decision when the timing is right. That timing is very individual.

MENTOR: *It was easy to see that here was a true martial artist. I have learned from some of the great Japanese masters in the true tradition of martial arts, and Georges was the first and only one I'd met who incarnated these beliefs, the way, the ryu, as we call it.*

I had a plan for him, and he accepted it with complete trust. In those early days, I'd travel across Canada and the U.S. regularly to give seminars, and even when I'd go out of town, I'd leave Georges with instructions and people to see for his training. He wanted this. And he'd do it without a doubt or a question. A lot of people say they train five hours a day, but it's not true, it's bullshit that they believe in their minds. Not him.

Standing still is never a good option. Not in the ring, and not in life outside the octagon either. When you stop moving, you're done. When the status quo becomes your main weapon, your arsenal is diminished. When you can find no other way forward except for repetition, your mistakes are compounded into defeat.

Therefore, the only way forward in life is innovation. And innovation, born from true creativity, depends on movement. Life, after all, is all about motion, whereas stasis is equivalent to death.

When you'd rather die than relive an error, and when you're truly committed to finding a better way to live your life, this is when the world opens its arms, welcomes and rewards you with opportunity. This is why we innovate, or we die.

Innovation is very important to me, especially professionally. The alternative, standing pat, leads to complacency, rigidity and eventually failure. Innovation, to me, means progression, the introduction of new elements that are functional and adaptable to what I do. It's all about making me better, whether through natural evolution or adaptation of previously unknown ideas. The reality is that innovation is a process, with its own rules and steps.

In my case, it's simple: I keep the white-belt mentality that I can learn from anyone, anywhere, anytime. For those of you who have never tried martial arts, the white-belt mentality is the first thing you understand, on your first day as a beginner when you receive your white belt: everything is knowledge, all must be learned. I try to maintain that mentality. When I discover an element that I think can be useful to me, I adapt it to my routine and my outlook; I submit it to a trial-error-and-refinement process. If it passes the test, I incorporate the new knowledge into my arsenal. I practice it and build up my muscle memory to perform it properly. I enter the octagon with an open, fresh mind, and with support from my handpicked team. And finally, I apply the innovation at the right time. It becomes who I am, and it means that innovation keeps me ahead of my competition. It means that my foes must adapt to me, not the other way around.

Another great reason to change training systems or approaches is to avoid boredom. Change is a great motivator, which is where all good training starts. When I get stuck doing the same things over and over again, I need something new or I start developing mental fatigue. I need to feel I'm constantly getting better.

That's why "innovate or die" rings true for me. My whole life, I've been fascinated by the natural world and how animals survive or become extinct. The study of dinosaurs is especially interesting because those creatures aren't here anymore, and they were the biggest, fiercest living things on the planet. Meanwhile, rats and cockroaches survive.

How is that? A cockroach can't defeat a dinosaur. But the cockroach is better at one thing, and it has ensured its survival through the ages: adaptation. One could adapt to the environment and the other one couldn't.

Most people don't realize this basic, fundamental and crucial thing, and it's key for mixed martial arts—and all sports, in fact. Your opponent constantly changes too. In the mixed martial arts world you fight wrestlers, grapplers, strikers. Every time you fight, your opponent doesn't look anything like the previous opponent. Taking it a step further, if it's the second time you fight an opponent, he often doesn't look like the previous version.

I fight knockout artists, grapplers, kickers, wrestlers, punchers—the whole gamut. I have to keep adapting to new hostile environments because what happens in the octagon is ever-changing. This is ingrained in my mind, and I've adapted my training to accept and prepare for it.

I believe that all the discussions I've had about history and dinosaurs and philosophy have made this possible. For some creatures, the match has already been settled. Today's creatures, well, we don't know who's coming out on top.

Right now, and for the next few years, I'll be in the midst of my struggle. So I can only be as good as a Boy Scout: *Toujours prêt*. Be prepared.

* * *

When I hurt my knee and needed surgery, my head coach, Firas Zahabi, said something very interesting. He explained that, in his mind, this injury is good because it will help define my career. He believes that if I come back and regain my title a third time, it will help make my career path and successes distinct from any other fighter's. It's an interesting point of view, and it has helped me focus my rehabilitation on clear goals I can visualize.

I've learned that my innovative capacities seem to rise up when there's a crisis, a conflict. Like losing my title, for example, or hurting my knee badly. Those situations told me I needed to continue my innovation to recapture my title, my place in martial arts. The way I see it, innovation is a discipline, not a lottery. It's got nothing to do with luck, or even eureka moments, because those are unplanned, unscripted. For me, it comes from the combination of two elements within my control: hard work and open-mindedness.

Very often, we see leaders lose sight of how they got to where they are: by being and thinking differently from the competition. They make it to first place, and then their thinking changes from seeking innovation to seeking the status quo. They think, *I made it to first place, so now I must not change a thing.* But change is what got them to the top in the first place! This is because they're focused on the positive result rather than on the *process* of success.

Innovation is why there are still human beings on the planet. The wheel, the plow, the harnessing of fire; religion, atheism, logic, mysticism; the longbow, gunpowder; modern medicine, the car, computer chips—the world is a constant reminder of the impact of innovation, whether through physical tools or intellectual theories or movements.

The history of war, for example, proves again and again that innovations are usually the deciding factor in battle. But this shouldn't be confused with inspiration: inspiration might be the initial idea or seed of the idea in a person's mind. Innovation means putting whatever the idea is through a process, checking results, using it in specific situations.

This is no different from my approach to fighting and the octagon, which is, in fact, my "battlefield." You can't simply enter and beat someone on instinct; you can't go in with the same approach over and over because it worked last time. Nowadays, every camp has access to video footage and has roughly the same technical tools as the opponent. The difference in success comes in the carefully planned innovation. You must change things up—not just keep them fresh, but progress. Your strategy might come as a surprise to the opponent, critics or fans, but in reality it has been well researched, learned and trained to a point that this innovation can then give way to inspiration.

Professional fighting, and mixed martial arts in particular, offers one of the least stable environments in terms of the sporting world. A fight is absolute, total, surreal chaos. The results fluctuate, and there are no safe returns in MMA, except winning.

All of my innovations are absolutely efficiency based. I take the risk of innovating, of building upon a winning formula to avoid becoming stale or complacent and, above all, to rise to the ever-changing challenge before me. If change is constant in the world, it must be for all individuals too.

MENTOR: *My being almost a decade older than Georges really helped both of us. I was able to help him avoid the mistakes I'd made, and he was open to accepting my word as bond. I explained in painstaking detail all the stupid things I did and mistakes I'd committed that had slowed or even harmed me, and I think it helped protect him from the same things.*

I never had a family, for example, so if I didn't fight, I didn't eat. This means that I often fought injured, and I shouldn't have. He never had to do that, he never had to fight injured to earn a square meal. He couldn't have and I wouldn't let him. Together, we could live day to day but keep an eye on the bigger, more important life goals. My mentality was this: I did what I had to do in my time, but

Georges I would treat like my little brother and protect him from my numerous mistakes.

One day, when Georges had been progressing nicely and attracting attention from professional fight promoters, Pete Spratt of the UFC came to Montreal. One of his goals was to have a good look at Georges, and people knew it. But Georges had hurt his knee in training, and despite this, he wanted to fight anyway. He wanted to make an impression. Both Georges and I were supposed to fight, and both of us were hurt, and I was going to fight anyway to make some money. He told me: "You're hurt and you're fighting anyway, so why wouldn't I? Why can't I be a warrior like you?" I tried to explain that I had to fight because I had no other choice. It was not about being a warrior, it was about choice.

It was a tough time. Georges had borrowed money from his mother and he wanted to pay her back. But I knew that we could fix those things. We could pool our money—that wasn't the issue. Everybody wanted Georges to fight that day, to get a shot at the big money, at the pros, but we had to keep our focus on the future.

I finally canceled my fight, out of solidarity with him. It was the dream day for a kid wanting to go to the UFC, but he didn't fight that day, either. We chose to wait. I'll never forget it: Georges had a tear in his eye. He felt bad and he sensed a chance was flying away. But I was sure that Spratt would come back another time. I explained to Georges that those people telling him to fight were people who had lost a major battle in their own lives, and weren't reconciled with it yet. They had no idea how their wishes were actually working against his better interests. They had had their one chance and they had missed it, and so they believed Georges couldn't miss this one. They were forecasting their regret onto his life.

But I told Georges: "You must not fight today. This way, you will fight another day." We waited. We waited, and it worked.

Kristof is an excellent fighter in his own right, one who could have been world champion, but while he's great at giving advice, to some he's not always as good at receiving it. Yet he lives his life *his* way, and I respect that.

MENTOR: *My reasons for testing Georges were simple: I'd explain to Georges that experience comes from the dojo and nowhere else. We didn't want our first real test to be on television; we wanted it to be right there in the dojo, every single day. That way, when he'd actually have to go out and fight in public, we'd both know whether or not he'd be truly ready. It wasn't always easy, and sometimes we disagreed, but not often, and I usually won the discussion and got the last word.*

It's very nice for me to be talking about fear and how it becomes powerful for you, but the consequence of facing your own fear is risk. Risk is unpredictable. If risk were predictable, every single investor in stocks or bonds would be a billionaire, and that's just not the case. What risk means is that sometimes, when you face your own fear, you may not win right away. You may struggle, and that means going backward. Or losing.

Without risk, though, there is no real reward; there's only luck, and I'm not planning on rolling the dice to decide the rest of my life. When I went to New Mexico to train with Greg Jackson before my second fight against Matt Serra, I was going out of my element completely and was taking risks on a number of levels. There was personal risk, because a lot of my local people were hurt that I was looking outside the usual borders for help. There was also professional risk, because down there I was just another guy in the gym, a small fish in a bigger pond.

When I announced to the media that I was about to have major surgery and be out of action for eight months, I took some really big risks. First of all, I said that belts don't matter to me, and that's risky because the people at the UFC have structured their whole business around belts. Second, I promised my fans that I wouldn't let them down and that I'd be world champion again. I promised them, in fact. That's a big risk.

The key for me, at this point in my life, is that I've climbed back up the mountain twice to regain my title. I know and understand what it takes to get back to that level. That's why I can take that kind of risk.

So what happens in life is that, as you grow and improve in whatever field you choose, so does the size of your challenges. So grows the size of the problems you can face and solve. Just two or three years ago, it wouldn't have been realistic to take that kind of risk. But now I feel it is me and me alone.

Risk comes in all shapes and colors: bankruptcy, heartbreak, failure. The alternative is a world without risk, without color, without knowing if you could have made that business work, if she would have truly loved you, if you would have finished that race or project or garden or painting or triathlon or . . . whatever. *If,* in other words, is risk's purgatory. I know I don't want to spend any time there.

It was *my* decision to make that announcement about regaining my title during my rehabilitation. I have a great team around me, and before that press conference we talked about the right things to say and how to say them, and what the right angle was and how to reassure people that everything was going to be okay. And that was very helpful to me, but when it came to stating, for me and my fans, that I would regain my title, that was my call alone because I'm the only person who 1) could truly *feel* it, and 2) has the right to *say* it.

The key to facing fear and taking risk is to start small. Get some practice and you'll discover you get better at facing fear. A really easy example is poker. A lot of people say they're good poker players, but if they understand anything at all about risk, they'll be very careful whose table they sit down at for a game, and how much money is at stake.

So what we're starting to understand here is that breaking down fear and evaluating risk is a step-by-step process.

MENTOR: *For months, I continued to test Georges and forced him to fight in the dojo before anything else. I'd say to him, "Here's what's going to happen—you'll come here tomorrow at this specific time, and other people will come too expecting a fight, and the one who has more capacity will win, and he will rise." I knew all along that the one who'd rise would be Georges, but he didn't know that. As for the other ones, unfortunately for them, they were bait. None of these people had the potential to become great champions. In no case did they have the potential, even though they looked very impressive, knocking fighters out on television. But a knockout is a deceptive thing, especially on a television screen. People fighting on TV, you don't see everything about them. But I'd fought with and trained all those people, I'd felt them and been around them, and only Georges stood out in my mind, in my gut. I'd lecture him, "Even that guy you saw on television, well, it's not reality. It's TV. You must discover the reality about that guy, and it's that you are more powerful than him."*

Georges just didn't have any choice. He'd get to the gym and see St-Louis there waiting for him, and he couldn't turn around. He couldn't leave, even if he wanted to.

Kristof and his partner, Stephan Potvin, massacred me for years. I felt every kind of pain imaginable, and more. I discovered places that could hurt that I didn't know existed. I understood what it means to be taken to the brink, to the limit. I survived some fantastically crazy stuff.

I'd get to the gym and I'd see Jason St-Louis on the mat, and he was waiting for me. I was seventeen years old! And yes, I was scared to death. But I also knew I needed to do this, I needed to pass these tests and understand that Kristof wouldn't let me get seriously hurt. Sometimes, he even had people waiting for me—it was totally nuts. He never told me ahead of time.

There were definitely times when I thought Kristof was crazy, and when I thought I was going to get my butt kicked. But I was sure it was part of his plan, so I needed to trust him and follow my instincts. I knew he wanted to grow my confidence.

MENTOR: *Yet, it was totally out of the question that we'd go out to Las Vegas for a cage fight without a clue as to what he could really do. We were surrounded by pretenders and big talkers who were constantly predicting how their own careers would flourish on the big stage. And we ignored them, choosing the dojo as the defining place, the first stage.*

We got to a point where we spent every moment of the day together—not only training together, but living in the same room together on these tiny beds in Georges's parents' basement. We shared a room, two small beds in the basement. We'd get up and go to the gym for some weightlifting and cardio—not all the stuff we do today. Then, later in the morning, we'd eat and talk about our training, and then we'd go to my gym in Montreal and practice Brazilian Jiu-Jitsu, and wrestling and other fighting disciplines, and then we'd go to our little beds and rest for a while, and then we'd go and eat some more. Later on, as the day progressed, we'd go to the local sports stadium in St-Isidore. In the winter, we'd wrap our feet in plastic bags and go running in the snow, around the track in fifty centimeters of slush. We just didn't care. We'd time ourselves, run like crazy, run like horses, in the dark around the track. We thought it was the right thing to do. We'd get home and finally we'd have no energy left, we were running on empty, so we'd jump into the ice-cold water outside in the above-the-ground pool, convinced it was good for our muscles (which it turns out it was). The water on some days had to be minus-2 or 3, and we'd break through a thinnish layer of ice, and we'd stay in for as long as we could.

Kristof stuck by me and was with me at the lowest: sweatpants, a thick winter coat, something to protect our faces from the frostbiting wind, a toque and a track in the dark, snow and slush halfway up our shins. I slept like a baby those nights. It's thanks to Kristof. He became like my big brother. We're like a family. He can walk into my house at any time and it's his house. My fridge is his fridge.

MENTOR: *His dad was convinced we had totally lost our minds. He'd say to me, "Tabarnak, mon fils peut pas faire ça!"—Christ, my son can't do that! And I'd reply that his son was strong and that he'd be a champion and he had no reason to worry. I spent months talking with Georges's dad. Every day, we'd talk and I'd go on about how I believed his son would be a champion. Neither he nor anyone else believed me—people just thought we were nuts. But I told him that if I was wrong, I'd be nothing but a buffoon. Everything we were doing just felt good and right.*

The first time I told my dad I wanted to be world champion in mixed martial arts, he thought I was nuts. It was my dream, sure, but everything begins with a dream, and it felt real inside my head. It was hard to talk about, and harder for others to understand or visualize. But I've always had premonitions, feelings and visions that felt like they belonged to me and me alone. Like the future sometimes takes place inside my head.

But this isn't a good thing if the future looks *bleak*. The loss to my hero Matt Hughes, for example. I saw it. From the stare-down, where I couldn't look at him and averted my eyes to the rafters. I'd lived the events inside my head long before the fight. I believed deep inside of me that I'd be champion someday, but I also felt this wasn't the right time.

The importance of the feeling, though, is that it put me on a path. Luckily, I know that each journey begins with one step, and is followed by another.

MENTOR: *The trick was accepting progress in small increments—a little bit at a time. He had to realize it. It's how he proved himself. He knew I was testing him, he knew what I was doing, but he never refused a fight. He comes from true, legitimate martial arts. He never said no and turned away. He did say, on a few occasions, "Wow, Kristof, that guy is really strong. Are you sure I should be fighting him?" And I'd tell him that if he didn't face and beat that guy today, there was no point in doing any of this. This wasn't the big time, it was just a step and he had to do it. He had to; it was an obligation.*

One of the lessons I learned in all those years of practicing karate is that progress only comes in small, incremental portions. Nobody becomes great overnight. Nobody crams information if he wants to be able to use it over the long term.

Confucius said: "Tell me and I'll forget. Show me and I'll remember. Involve me and I'll understand." I love that quote, and I'm lucky to have had teachers throughout my career who understood new ways of involving me in learning.

It's like the concept of *kaizen*. *Kaizen* is the Japanese philosophy of continuous, slow improvement. It's about finding smarter ways of working instead of just harder ways of working. I'm definitely not an expert on *kaizen*, not in the least. But Rodolphe Beaulieu, a very close friend and my old Brazilian Jiu-Jitsu training partner, keeps telling me that I am living the life of *kaizen*, that I invented my career by following the *kaizen* path. He describes it like this:

> *Kaizen is a little bit like the white-belt mentality. You listen to what everybody around you says about a subject, any subject, and from those opinions you form your own and take the best solution-path possible. You don't have to think of everything, because a great idea can come from anywhere. There are two kinds of suggestion boxes: the ones that are opened and the suggestions are read, and the ones that are opened so the opinions can be tossed aside, unread.*

One example, dieting, is probably the place where I see the least *kaizen* thinking. We all know people who spend two or three months essentially starving themselves to lose weight— only to gain most of it back with a couple of binge sessions. But there are much better ways of taking on a mission. Don't think of the mountain, think of the first thousand steps. Think of the low-hanging fruit.

This is incredibly important because a great physical journey is only possible if your mentality is nourished with positive energy. It's going to feel good to reach that first plateau, and what happens is that the second plateau is even easier to reach, and more gratifying. Performance improves. Results are tangible. Your mind and your body feel better and are finally working in harmony.

In other words, when you prepare a list of improvements and you make them small and achievable, you won't just stick to them, you'll increase the chances that you'll keep going forward.

Another point of view that relates to this approach comes from a samurai named Yamamoto Tsunetomo. In his classic samurai manifesto *Hagakure,* he writes: "Matters of great concern should be treated lightly. Matters of small concern should be treated seriously."

In other words, when you pay attention to detail, the big picture will take care of itself. The way I see it, details are everywhere and in everything people say. Ninety-nine opinions are one better than ninety-eight—but only if you're listening to everything people express. In the past five years, for example, my arm bar has gotten better. It was pretty good when I started my career, but now it's a much better, smarter weapon because I've kept on trying to improve it.

Since Rodolphe is a good old friend of mine, I've tried to understand why he sees *kaizen* in what he calls my "way." What do I see? I see a lot of people working themselves harder than they ever have, but without any chance of obtaining the desired result. And that's because of their overall approach.

Think about climbing a mountain. If you decide you're going up Everest, you don't start with a sprint. You'll never make it out of base camp if you do that. The secret is twofold: make sure your approach is consistent and steady so that you can maintain the progress you're making as your journey continues.

MENTOR: *Every day, Georges got better. I weighed 240 pounds and he didn't, and every day I martyred him and he never* *complained. Not once, not ever. He just kept coming back. I didn't try to hurt him in any way possible, but I put pressure on him at the right moments in the right places so he could feel, process and understand the full extent of pain. A fighter must understand the pain he inflicts on another if he is to know any success at all.*

Martyrdom for me meant taking him to the threshold of pain without ever breaking anything. It's what the Russians do. The Japanese too. I took him to the limit because that's when we'd discover how mad he really is. He could have been physically strong but weak-willed, which means one day he would have broken. But because he's traditional and proud, he never even dared tell me "I'm tired" or "I'm hurting."

Even though I make the process sound simple, I have often struggled. The Matt Serra loss is a great example. It was my first title defense, and I didn't prepare for it right. Serra was an 11–1 underdog. Nobody thought he had a chance against me. And I believed them. I thought I was invincible. I thought I was going to easily kick his butt. We spent six weeks sparring and training together as part of an *Ultimate Fighter* TV show, yet I *still* underestimated his skills and his power. In fact, I didn't believe he even deserved to be in the octagon, challenging me for the title I had won not so long before. In truth, I believed what people were saying: that I was the greatest fighter of all time in my category.

And what happened?

Well, it turned out it *was* easy. Matt Serra kicked my ass. And he did it in under two minutes. I tried to duck the blow but got stunned. It was a shot to the back of the head—which, done intentionally, is illegal, but I had caused it, and instead of steadying my emotions and regaining my calm and my senses, I lost all of my composure. The first thought in my blurry head was *I need to hit him hard and show everybody my superiority,* but I was so shaken up that there was no precision in any of my counterstrikes. But he sure knew where and how to hit me. And so that first shot to my head triggered a domino effect in Serra's favor.

Serra is known for his grappling. He doesn't have a reputation as a lethal striker or a big puncher, so I wasn't expecting that from him. I ignored any danger of him standing right in front of me. That was half the problem—forgetting what I had learned so many years before on that snowy mountain: the element of surprise. The other half was that I didn't react well to the surprise either. When he first rocked me, I should have stepped back, caught my breath and protected myself. I should have retreated and reorganized. I should have focused on regaining my composure. But instead, I followed my emotional impulse and went for it.

I wanted to knock him out. I missed with my counter and exposed my head. This isn't good at the best of times, especially for a fighter like me who tries to *avoid* getting hit. So he immediately put five or six shots straight on me, one after the other—*bang-bang-bang-bang-bang*—a nice combination, and then I went down to the mat. And there I was, lying on my back with Matt Serra on top of me, about to strip me of my title. When I went down I had no idea where I was. All I knew was that I was in major trouble. I had no choice but to tap out.

So what really killed me was my pride. I've taken bigger shots from better punchers—people like Josh Koscheck, for example, who can really strike some big blows. But I was expecting those shots because they were known strikers. But for Serra, the pride I brought into the cage reacted before my mind could, and I lost. Now, when my team and I prepare for a fight, we not only plan for every possible scenario, which I replay in my head repeatedly, but I also keep my pride in check.

It didn't get better in the moments right after the Serra fight. I was stunned and alone in the center of the octagon. Leaning my head against a towel, I could only feel shame. Shame for letting everybody down, for failing myself and for deceiving my fans. I just wanted to find a place where I could hide, where no one would see me. It was a horrible feeling. And then Rodolphe walked into the octagon and came straight to me. I looked up at him and said, "Rodolphe, this is the worst day of my life." I meant it too.

MENTOR: *I pushed his limits, and I couldn't believe how much he could take. I'd see the tears well up in the corners of his eyes, but he stayed silent. He never complained. He just kept treating me respectfully. To me, this meant that he'd never refuse to enter the ring out of fear. I knew that just with a look or a word, he'd hold his head high, fear or not. He showed me what real courage was, which meant that I had a responsibility to him. To help him learn and shine.*

For weeks and months after this fight, all I could think about was revenge. It was a waste of energy. I knew—or should have known—that I wouldn't get a shot at revenge straight away. I'd have to earn it. I'd have to fight other lesser challengers before getting a chance. It would take time, and patience.

But Serra wouldn't leave my thoughts. He haunted me for a long time. I had steps to go through before getting back to where I needed to go.

Luckily for me, I talked about it. A friend of mine told me it was like I was carrying a brick with me every day, everywhere I went. And the thing about carrying a brick is that it gets heavier and heavier with time. My buddy's proposed solution was to actually get a real brick, write Serra's name on it, and carry it everywhere with me. This way I'd realize the kind of weight I was carrying with me everywhere, and the amount of energy it took to keep it slung onto my shoulder.

And so I literally got the brick and wrote down his name. I took it with me for car rides to the gym. I carried it in my bag. When I went to bed, I placed it on the desk just outside my door, so that the moment I walked out of my room in the morning, I'd see it and be reminded of it.

I carried that darn thing all over the place. I'd see and feel its weight all the time, and it was driving me nuts. It really bothered me. The easy thing would have been to throw it away, but that would have been a short-term solution. I couldn't get rid of it by pretending. If I was being honest with myself, I knew I had to keep it for a while. I could have played a game and tossed it away, but that would have been untrue. The demons were still there, and I couldn't afford to do that. I learned you have to let the trick work on you, and it takes time.

Then something magical happened. Josh Koscheck began trash-talking.

At a certain point I realized that, slowly, I'd naturally begun focusing more on Koscheck than on Serra. It was perfect. Without realizing it as it happened, my mind was slowly putting Serra behind me and bringing all of my attention to Koscheck. It was being logical and diverting my energy away from the emotional loss to Serra.

One night, I looked at the brick and knew it was time. I don't know how to explain it except that I just knew, I felt it in my gut. So I got in my car and drove from Nuns' Island, where my condo is, to Île Ste-Hélène, just outside downtown

Montreal. It was dark, but the moon was so bright it cut my shadow into the sidewalk. I found a spot on the bridge and observed the light hitting the water, moving in waves. I took a long look around and confirmed that I was alone. I got the brick out of my bag, held it up and took one last good look at Serra's name. And then I reached my arm back, hurled it forward in a long loop, and tossed that brick as far away as I could. I watched it hit the water—*SPLASH!*—and sink away where nobody would ever find it. And with it went the demon of Matt Serra.

It felt really good. It was total deliverance. And it was immediate.

Eventually, the loss taught me a new kind of patience. It showed me the value of waiting for the right opportunity and accepting life's cycle. It gave me the time to acquire knowledge about myself to prevent my losing to Serra ever again.

MENTOR: *People, fans mostly, don't understand the professional Georges, the champion who keeps winning. They see him in the ring for a twenty-five-minute fight and they complain that he didn't do much. Well, they have no idea what they're talking about. First of all, Georges is the champion. Second, inside the ring he's an assassin, a killer, but he can't show you that side all the time. When he's training he can show you how feeble and weak and ridiculous you are as an opponent, because he can afford to. In the ring during a fight, he cannot do that. People don't understand that. In the octagon, it's payday that's coming, it's his job, and that job, first and foremost, is to win. It's great if we can earn a payday and make people happy, but it's not the top priority. That day, he's risking his life. And if he loses, everybody leaves him behind. People forget that. If Georges loses* *tomorrow, people will say he's done. These people have no idea what the word spectacular means.*

At the beginning of my career, my style was much more physical and much less technical, which is natural: I was very naive and didn't have a great amount of knowledge or wisdom. As I progressed, losses to Serra and Hughes forced me to ask myself what I was doing wrong.

Throughout my career, I've compensated a lot with my athleticism. Sometimes I've just overpowered guys. That's a natural advantage, and I'd never discount that one. I'm a good athlete and I can win with that sometimes, but if I had made this a staple of my strategy, I would never have been a good *champion*. It would have been a short-term mentality to try and compensate for a mental absence of vision.

Genetics and athleticism can be a blessing, but for some they can be a curse. If you're physically so gifted that you don't need a lot of effort to be the best when you're young, you can lose out on learning the tough lessons that the little brothers and sisters learn. If it's always easy, it's hard to believe that one day it's going to get harder. Young people at some point need to be tested, because their reaction will determine their path. So genetics is good to those who combine it with a mental outlook aimed at understanding the growth potential in struggle, defeat and hunger.

MENTOR: *Only an idiot constantly tries to knock the other guy out. But to destroy an opponent by repeatedly striking him in the same place over twenty-five minutes, that's genius. That's a champion. Not everyone can do that. True sportsmen understand the difference.*

I've been down a number of times in my life, but I was ten years old the first time I knocked somebody out. It was on some street corner in St-Isidore, and this kid was giving me a hard time. He wanted to fight, to hit me. He grabbed my shoulders and was trying to yank me down hard, stiffly. I kicked him in the stomach. I kicked as hard as I could, lunging forward, and made a direct contact. I remember the *oomph*. He went straight down.

That was the first time, and I'll always remember that feeling.

When you really connect with another human being, when you really hit your opponent fully, the most impressive part of the act isn't actually the impact. Many people are quite mistaken when they think the connection is the thing. The recoil's the thing.

Feet determine where you position your body laterally and how you move in relation to the octagon and your opponent. But then your feet have to connect with your brain, and the way they do that is through your eyes.

The eyes determine the punching angle, another very key element in a successful fight. I got to learn that from an unsuccessful fight against Matt Serra. Serra has a very strong overhand right punch. When I fought him the first time, I fought tall, and that was a bad idea. When you fight tall against a shorter opponent with a strong right punch, you open yourself (and the entire left flank of your head) to his strength because you're punching down. You leave nothing to protect yourself and that's what happened against Serra. I got tagged, repeatedly. Thanks to this defeat, though, I learned about punching angles, which I never used to pay attention to.

The key is always being lined up with your opponent's eyes, like you're trying to stay on a level with a wave in the ocean. Up and down, side to side, stay level with his eyes. Like he's your prey. When you stay lined up with his eyes, you punch straight out instead of down, which increases the power of your impact, maximizes your reach and lets your shoulder protect your face from his overhand right.

It's basic geometry, really, and most of you learned that early on in high school. So take a right-angle triangle, turn it on its side so the hypothenuse points from the ground to your opponent, and you'll see how your eye-level punch is both efficient and direct. Anything else is a lack of productivity.

As a fighter progresses, again, he or she develops the right to play with the rules and turn them to his or her advantage. When I fight an overhand puncher now, I tend to crouch down. When I fight a good kicker, I will often stand taller. You have to know your opponent, not just yourself. Fighting Matt Hughes, for example, isn't the same thing as fighting Josh Koscheck. Hughes can slam you down like a basketball, while Koscheck can knock you out with a single overhand right. The difference isn't subtle, it's lethal. After landing the strike cleanly, as you pull away, you can feel all of his energy draining out of his body. Like you've opened a wound. You can sense all of his force pouring out of his body. You can feel a surge, and your entire being realizes that the opponent has been defeated, absorbed in a single blow. His soul, all his energy, gone—*poof!*—just like that. In one connection.

When I look back at my knockouts in MMA, the guys I've finalized in professional fights are guys who came in strong against me. Not even Koscheck tried that, not against me. He knew better. A lot of people complained that I didn't open up my power game against him. Well, neither did he. He didn't take any risks, so why should I have taken them?

MENTOR: *Georges's intellect is unique. He is more than my student, he is my teacher. He has given me back so much* *learning and wisdom. When I left for Korea for a fight one time, I got on the plane and flew for twenty-four hours. I was tired, empty. I got there and climbed into the ring, but I'd lost the desire to fight. I wanted to leave, to be elsewhere. On the day of the fight, I sat alone in my dressing room and I pulled on the gloves, but I was down. When it came to my turn, I didn't feel like it. But then I heard those fans cheering against me. Some threw objects at me, cans, and when I heard that and heard them wanting to see me get hurt, I thought of Georges. I thought of the things we'd learned together. I thought, Wow, you won't get to do this tomorrow, or later on, or in a little while. It's now. Sleep will come later, but this you must face now. Go do what you have to do. And if you get destroyed in fifteen minutes, that'll be that. But I exploded that guy. It took less than a minute and I destroyed him completely. Afterward, I slept and ate and went home.*

A sports journalist told me two stories about athletes he has written about in his life. The first was about Maurice "Rocket" Richard, the greatest hockey player who ever lived. The Rocket scored over five hundred goals during his career, and was the first man ever to score fifty goals in fifty games. What he accomplished was unbelievable.

My journalist friend was telling me that the Rocket used to spend a lot of time alone on the ice at the Montreal Forum, practicing his shot. One day, a television crew came to film him, and they asked him, "Rocket, what's the secret for scoring all those goals?"

Rocket stopped what he was doing and looked at them, and then he said, "I shoot the puck at the net." Then he got the bucket of pucks out and started shooting pucks at the net. They all went in. That was his great secret.

The other story was about Mike Strange of Niagara Falls, a great amateur Canadian boxer who won gold medals for Canada at the Commonwealth Games. It was 1998 and my journalist friend was writing a feature about Strange during the Commonwealth Games in Kuala Lumpur, Malaysia. Strange was known as a technician, a scientific boxer, and my friend wanted to write a story about that, the precision and the art of boxing. So he asked a long question about technicalities and science, because he wanted Strange to talk about the scoring system in boxing and how to win on the scorecards.

Strange looked at him and said, "Hit and don't get hit. *That's* how you win a fight."

So the geometrists can discuss triangles and Pythagoras and his theorem all they want, but please never forget that a big part of it is really simple. It's a straight line and it's right in front of your eyes, so just follow it.

MENTOR: *Georges is always willing to go out. He's always the first one in the ring, the last one out. He's the last one in the showers but the first to be by the door, clean, dressed and ready to go. He always makes time for life. He trains three hours, then he eats and finishes with an enormous chocolate cake so you think you're home free and you can relax, but then he says, "We have to hurry to the next training session and start before digestion begins or else we're screwed." And then your spirit fails and you can't believe he's still going. And then he goes to lift weights and do jumping jacks or some other insane activity, and then you go eat again. He takes you to an oyster bar or something and you think, Okay, THIS time we're okay because nobody can eat oysters and then train, again. But then you finish eating and he takes you to yoga. And so you think, It's yoga, how bad can it be? But he takes you to* *some goddamn hot-room yoga for two hours at night after oysters, and while you're puking your oysters into the garbage can, he's just going through the exercises and stretching.*

Another fighter who reads this story will see himself and the one time he got up and decided he was too tired or too sore to train. The money's in the bank. It can get done tomorrow. One day off won't hurt. Whatever the excuse is, it exists. But not for Georges.

It's really not about how much weight you can lift over your head. If your prime movers can generate five hundred pounds of pressure, but your stabilizers can only support one hundred pounds of pressure, you're in trouble. In a worst-case scenario, you may only move a hundred pounds. This is not good at all, because there are rarely any good-case scenarios in the heat of intense, top-level competition. As soon as your stabilizers are outmatched, the whole house of cards is going to come down, hard. This means total collapse, and often the result is injury, epic failure, or both.

If you can squat a ton and bench-press five hundred pounds and you don't believe me, go running across an ice rink. Try to reach full speed, and then try to stop. You can't. You can't, but your amazing strength is still there. What is it doing for you? Nothing. The ice doesn't let you generate any force. Balance, on the other hand, equals stability. Stability, in this case, is about getting a grip. So get a grip first.

The same is true in martial arts. To me, for example, Brazilian Jiu-Jitsu is the science of using mechanical forces and leverage instead of pure physical strength. So one of the things I've been doing in training is to kick and punch into the high pads while standing on a balancing board. The key is to maintain balance while generating power.

True power is generating force from all positions, in all situations.

MENTOR: *He does everything he wants to do, he'll have fun all night if he wants to, but then he'll train. He's even tricked me into it once.*

We were in London at a training camp, and on the Saturday night, after three insane days of training, he told me: "Kristof, let's go out tonight, let's get loose and have fun, and tomorrow we'll skip the workout. We've done enough this week, so tonight we party and drink vodka." I remember thinking, Great. At long last, I get to have a few drinks, and we did.

But at five in the morning, when we're heading back to our hotel, he grabs my shoulder and pulls me in and says, "Hey, Kristof, I lied to you about something."

"What about?" I asked.

"Well, just know that I did it for your own good . . . But if I'd told you all those hours ago that on Sunday morning we'd still be training, and that the television cameras are coming to film the sparring session tomorrow, and that you'll be Royce Gracie's sparring partner in the ring, you'd have never come out with us to party."

I couldn't believe it, I went nuts! "Mon esti de tabarnak," I said, swearing in the French-Canadian dialect. I was drunk, tired and worried. So I went to the bathroom and stuck my finger down my throat, and he just told me not to worry so much. I threw up, we slept an hour, we got up, I felt like crap, we did our sparring and training, we put on a good show, and then we went to eat and sleep. I learned something from him: that if he only had his regimen and his discipline, he'd not have any life in him. He needs to go out and live those moments because they confirm his humanity. This guy has been able to combine a great personal life with the requirements of life as champion, even drunk at 5 a.m. I've tried to keep up with him and his going-out habits, but I can't do it. Not like him. Nobody I've known can.

And now that he's champion and the best in the world, he's even worse. It's like a boss who gets to the office before all of the staff and stays late at night to be sure he sees the door close at the end of the day—he's obsessed.

Georges's secret is no secret at all. He just has to get up every morning and go to work. Like any other businessman. I have never seen him miss a day of training. Not once has he said, "Hey, I'm tired," or "I'm hurt," or "I'm not sure," or "This part of my body is in pain, let's take today off." We've never postponed a workout. We've acted like we've had nothing else to do, since forever. He hasn't moved from this position by a centimeter—he's had the same dedication, and now it's even better because he's grown. He's more precise. Before, we didn't really know what to do; we just did whatever came up. Now he knows. Georges knows he's alone in this.

I just wouldn't be where I am without Kristof. He's my first *sensei*. A true *ronin*. His life is extraordinary. He was an inspiration for me. He had so many obstacles against him, he never got the chance to be a champion. I believe he would have been a great champion; he could have made it. But he paid for his mistakes, and he paved the way for me.

MENTOR: *In the time it takes a good athlete to have one good workout in the gym, he's put himself through three different training sessions. And he's showered, and he's out before you. I've observed him do it—here's how it goes: while people were*

Even on my bike I was a martial artist.

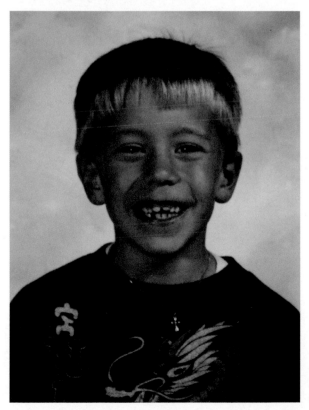

Eight years old and dreaming of ninjas.

My best friend when I was growing up.

My sister blocking me much too easily.

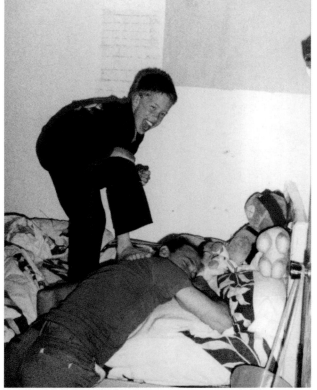

"Submitting" dad.

As a kid, my idol was Wayne Gretzky, "The Great One."

Proudly showing my first black belt, with my sensei Jean Couture.

Becoming a mixed martial artist with Kristof Midoux.

Celebrating my first championship belt (UCC) with my mom.

With Kristof—even the toughest warriors have a gentle side!

My first weigh-in as a UFC fighter with my opponent, Karo Parisyan (*left*), and UFC President Dana White (*center*). JOHANN VAYRIOT/KARATÉ BUSHIDO

Ready to fight Matt Serra again at UFC 83. ERIC WILLIAMS

Relieved and happy after regaining my championship belt at UFC 83—I'm back!

A gift from the UFC that made my father, Roland, very happy.

From St-Isidore to hanging out at the Grammy Awards.
JON KOPALOFF/FILMMAGIC/GETTY IMAGES

Another day at work at the Tristar Gym! ELIDA ARRIZZA/SID LEE

warming up and chatting, nobody saw Georges do exercises with two other guys for fifteen, twenty minutes. Then he did the big training with the group and, when everybody else goes to the shower, he does another individual training session for about twenty minutes. And then he somehow grabs his bag and showers and is ready to go before everyone else. And if you don't watch him intently, you don't notice it. I've been watching him for years. He takes everything you throw at him, and then he does more. He pushes himself harder than even you can in your own mind. Think about that.

Kristof was a true legend where I came from. MMA wasn't a big deal in those days, and there weren't a lot of international guys like Kristof, guys with knowledge and experience and wisdom. I knew I wanted to train with the very best available, and he was the only one at his level, so when I saw him walking down the street that day, on St-Laurent in downtown Montreal, I had to chase him. To be honest, I've always kind of wondered why he took me in. I think it's because he's just naturally a nice, generous person.

BOOK 3

MASTER

The Transition Book

WITH

JOHN DANAHER, BRAZILIAN JIU-JITSU TEACHER

After hearing I needed that surgery, I felt the fear as it took over my body, my brain, my being.

felt it in my gut, an ugly, shitty feeling, and I sensed it creeping up and tightening my chest and squeezing my throat. I don't know how I remained standing. I don't know if I leaned on the wall or sat in a chair or started walking toward a door so I could breathe, I was so overwhelmed.

I went down the list of horrible thoughts. I started wondering if I was ever going to fight again. If I would ever defend my title again. If I would ever stand in front of my fans and feel the rush I get from their screams. If I would ever fight the way I know I can, the way I always have, the only way I know how. I saw myself slowing down, getting hit. I sensed a loss in impact, in rhythm, in timing. I wouldn't explode into an opponent ever again. No more Superman punch. No more takedowns. No more submissions. No more grappling or wrestling or lunging or evading. No more fighting. Or winning. No more champion. No more me.

All these things flashed through my mind at that fearful moment.

Fear, once you get used to it, can be mastered. You can tame fear, and I knew that. It can take some time and you can go through some pretty bad moments, but at some point fear is going to get tired or overconfident, and you can take it down. But this wasn't that time.

MASTER: *A good way to understand my first meeting with Georges St-Pierre is to understand its mundane nature. I was teaching a beginner's class at Gracie's Gym in New York City. Georges came in and was immediately conspicuous by his lack of English. He was only a blue belt in those days, relatively inexperienced. He joined in, clumsily, but with enthusiasm. He had what I would describe as above-average athletic potential, but by no means was he spectacular. I've had numerous athletes with far greater ability than him.*

I was seventeen years old, I had just arrived in New York City, I didn't have any money and I was intimidated. I was going into a crack neighborhood, before the cleaner years. It wasn't a full-on ghetto, but I'd never seen that kind of place. But I walked in there, into the Gracie gym, seeking knowledge. They let me in.

MASTER: *At the end of the drilling session, we commenced live training. Students would face off against each other. At that point in his career, Georges applied himself well against the beginners, but his overall skill was unexceptional. When he rolled with more advanced athletes, he was overwhelmed. But he was not intimidated. Rather, he seemed delighted by it. Most people, when they encounter defeat, experience a diminishing in their enthusiasm. Yet, as Georges encountered defeat, his enthusiasm only grew.*

I couldn't speak a lick of English, and every fighter in the place wanted a go at me, the new guy. That's the way it is in a gym—a real fighting gym. A new guy walks in and everybody wants a shot at him. I got my ass kicked many times. The kind of practice we participated in is called *randori*. Essentially, it means freestyle practice of one-on-one sparring. The goal is to resist and counter the opponent's techniques. The Japanese translation of the word *randori* is "chaos-taking," or "grasping freedom." Well, they almost fought over me. I suffered my share of whoopings. I ate a lot of *randori,* let's say. I was really discouraged at first, but I went there to learn Brazilian Jiu-Jitsu, to learn the art of fighting on the ground from the experts. Those guys really are the best in the world.

> **MASTER:** *Many of us, when we picture the meeting of great people at some pivotal point in their lives, we picture great events taking place. But this was noteworthy only in that it wasn't noteworthy at all. A random beginner's class, on a random day, during an unexceptional month. If anyone had walked into that class and seen the people rolling, there was not even a single thing that suggested that they were witnessing the early career of one of the greatest martial artists of all time. Nothing he did that first day was memorable. Nothing.*

I found out a lot of things about myself that first day: mostly that I could get my ass kicked really good. I've had my butt handed to me many times in that place. I'm definitely not the king of that gym. But that's why it's so good.

If anything, I don't ever want to start by being the king. It doesn't work that way. A person can't be good from the beginning. You have to go through the stages of learning, the tests, and learn from them. You need to grow. These guys had been doing this a long time, and on the day I got there, I didn't *want* to beat them. I wanted to work hard and learn from them so that I could improve.

At John's dojo, there was a guy named Sean Williams. After I'd been there a few times, he called me over and told me I was very raw material, very athletic, and that he felt he could do something with me. So I chose to believe and trust him. He said all I was missing was technique. This was tough to hear for me because I was used to "taking care" of guys much bigger than me in Montreal—it really put a dent in the ego. My pride suffered hugely.

But it wasn't just talk. In those days, despite the fact that he was smaller than me, when he and I fought, Sean would easily finalize me six or seven times in five minutes. That's more than once a minute, which is clearly inferior and pathetic. And to top off the humiliation, my girlfriend at the time—who had come to New York a couple of times and watched us spar—told me Sean was very good-looking. Let's just say I started going to New York alone after that trip.

But Sean was the only guy who didn't target me; his students did that. Despite finalizing me so easily so many times, Sean was the one telling me not to be discouraged because he could see in my eyes that I was losing hope. I was ready to quit, but he caught me just in time. We're still friends and we train together when I'm in Los Angeles. I affectionately call him my worst nightmare. He still can't believe I almost quit back in the day, and he still reminds me of that all the time!

Humility is the first rule of martial arts. Either you learn humility quickly, or you leave because your ego can't handle losing repeatedly. I don't like losing—nobody does, especially in front of your girlfriend or your buddies (or millions of people watching on pay-per-view television). But it's good to realize you're not always as strong as you thought. It's good in the long run.

MASTER: *Everyone begins at the bottom, even someone as talented as Georges. No one who witnessed that meeting would have guessed that they were looking at a future superstar. Our initial meeting shows just how far a human being can progress through the combination of will and time. Georges St-Pierre is possessed of a tremendously strong will.*

John Danaher eats only once a day. He trains seven days a week in eight-hour stretches. I don't know why. He's just that way. He's the cleverest person I know. A true intellectual, a singularly interesting man, and just a special person.

MASTER: *He was coming by bus, nine, ten hours from Montreal, to study Brazilian Jiu-Jitsu. He was staying in dilapidated and physically uncomfortable living conditions, in flophouses across various New York ghettos. He shared rooms with people who smoked drugs. He was coming to a country where he spoke almost nothing of the language. On a garbageman's salary and at considerable personal expense, he was seeking to better himself. That points immediately to the strength of his will and the strength of his vision. I didn't learn that on the first day, but I learned it soon enough, in the coming weeks and months.*

The very first time I was in New York City, I lasted two days. So that's how I timed every other visit. I'd drive down from Montreal whenever I had three consecutive days off. Usually, I'd stay in this horrible hostel, and I'll never forget it because I once shared a room with six kids visiting from Holland, and they'd smoke pot in the room all the time. It drove me nuts, and my *gi* smelled like weed, so I got angry one day and kicked them out of the room. I mean, I'd go to train and I smelled like a pot plant— all the guys in the gym teased me, it was terrible.

But I went to New York for a reason. Throughout my life, I've tried to continue on my knowledge path. I was lucky to understand early on that there were always more coaches in the world that I could learn from. Training with John Danaher and the Gracie family was of paramount importance. Renzo Gracie is a legend in our sport; the family's legacy is without equal.

In those days, every dollar I made went to my training. I knew it would pay off; I just felt it. My expenses were gas, hotels, food and classes. I think it was $20 a day—nothing, really, when you think of it, when you think of what Brazilian Jiu-Jitsu gave me in return. Nothing, even though in those days I calculated my life in $5 increments.

I made it into a game. Someone had told me that following trucks was a good way to save on gas, so I'd follow trucks from Montreal to New York to save a few bucks on fuel. Eventually, I started timing my New York trips with Rodolphe, who would go in for work meetings. He'd fly and I'd drive. I'd sleep on the floor of his hotel room and train while he went to his meetings. I made it my goal to go there as much as possible and saturate my brain with all the best Brazilian Jiu-Jitsu knowledge anywhere in the world.

MASTER: *When most people are asked to explain what makes Georges different, most talk about his athletic ability. They say he's a freak of nature, built out of muscle, and it's his athleticism that makes him the best. I'll tell you straight: Georges is above average in athleticism, but he's nothing special. If Georges went to an NFL combine, he'd just be another guy. In fact, he'd be below the average at that level. Good jumping ability and explosiveness, but nothing crazy. I've seen many people with a better vertical jump than him. He has average endurance. Decent but not great flexibility.*

Average balance. He's overall a good—but not great—athlete. No, it's not his athleticism.

I'm fortunate to have a memory geared to my chosen profession. I can remember every single important detail of a fight and I can replay each moment in my head. My mind has always been like that. And then there are things my body does that are inexplicable but to me are second nature.

The brain has to be accustomed to being coordinated. This is how it learns to execute the movement. The brain must assimilate the movement before it can properly think of using it. The Superman punch? It starts with a fake kick, a hop, and is followed by a lunging punch. But it's more than pure athleticism, as athleticism is traditionally defined.

Phil Nurse taught me the Superman punch. I'd had it in the arsenal for a number of years—every true fighter does—but I'd never got it right. Between my fights against Penn and Hughes, I was at Phil's gym in New York—called The Wat, which means "temple" in Thai—and Phil saw straight away that there was nothing *super* in my technique. So he showed me, step by step, and we both soon discovered that it would become an important weapon in my repertoire.

The Superman punch is one of the good examples of how I try to fool my adversary, to keep him guessing. It's a great tool because it's not part of most fighters' codes (more on "codes" later). Most fighters are not accustomed to seeing it in practice, and that affects the brain's reaction time. They don't recognize it well. It's the kind of maneuver that starts in one body part but finishes in another. Tactically, there are at least six ways to start the move, and ten different endings. You can begin with a takedown feint and finish with a punch—it doesn't matter how or where it starts, because it can end in so many ways.

People think athleticism is just physical, but it's not. It's connected to the brain and how the brain can learn to execute and see a movement or not. Especially at high speed. Being athletic is not just jumping and running and being powerful. It's the the nervous system that guides the body. The muscles don't decide anything. The brain decides and makes things happen.

MASTER: *Georges is the hardest-working athlete I ever knew. But he's hardly the only guy out there with good work ethic. Almost every guy out there works hard. Jon Fitch is notorious and probably, in terms of hours, outworks Georges, yet we all know what happened when they met. It's not just his work ethic that makes his great; it's his depth of insight that gives direction to his work that makes him great.*

It was my favorite fight. Fitch kept on attacking me. He just kept on coming. No matter what I did, no matter what happened, no matter where I hit him or how hard, he kept coming. He's the most resilient opponent I've ever faced.

I saw him coming too. I saw his face and what he was thinking. I was faster and stronger that day, I was always a step ahead of him, but he refused to accept it. He refused to accept my dominance. He refused it by relentlessly moving forward, one step at a time. And I hit him. I hit him with my right, and his jaw jutted away from his face, and the sweat leaped off his head into midair, and he staggered back, stunned. I watched him.

Some opponents, you break their will and they lose their desire. They no longer try. They no longer can. The fight is gone out of them. They are defeated and waiting for the fatal blow.

Not Jon Fitch. He never broke.

Repeatedly, I hit him hard, and it shook his entire body. He shook, but I could never let my guard down. I knew he'd be capable of anything. So when I hit him, well and hard and directly, and he staggered back, I did not pounce, I did not leap. I evaluated. I calculated the proper next steps and carried on with my plan. Because that is the way of my fight. There are fights when you feel like you're in a bubble. The world evaporates and slows as every gesture, every movement, is performed correctly. It feels perfect in terms of execution, even though perfection is impossible. This was, at moments, one of these fights.

Fitch kept coming. And for every single attack, I returned an answer.

MASTER: *If I asked you to run through a brick wall, it would be hard work, not smart work. It wouldn't make you better. Hard work doesn't necessarily garner results, and hard, stupid work gives you negative results. As the great Benjamin Franklin once said, "Never mistake movement for action."*

Bruce Lee is one of the greatest martial artists there ever was. He was the first to try and accomplish so many new things. He took the word *artist* beyond the known boundaries of the word. Bruce, for example, was the first to train his muscles not for power but for functionality. He understood very early on that real physical power complements other skills that are more important, like strategy and technique. He believed that total fitness was the perfect combination of many things: flexibility, strength and a strong respiratory system. He found that real strength was found in connective tissue—which holds muscles on the human frame—more than muscle size or muscle mass. In fact, Bruce Lee believed that bigger muscles could actually be bad for martial artists because they limit movement and fluidity. He saw that big muscles actually make people slower and reduce their mobility. For Bruce, everything had to be fluid.

Fluidity made Bruce Lee who he is, and had a huge impact on my development too. It shows the human and philosophical side of the ultimate martial artist. Here's something he said about being fluid:

Empty your mind, be formless, shapeless, like water. If you put water into a cup, it becomes the cup. You put water into a bottle, it becomes the bottle. You put it into a teacup, it becomes the teacup. That water can flow, or it can crash. Be water, my friend.

I've learned that a thing is perfect only if it's perfect for you. For me, that comes from being fluid, from being open to ideas and better ways of doing things. Think of Bruce and the water analogy: sometimes you can see through water, and other times it clouds and you can't see anything. Sometimes water can drill through the hardest surfaces, while other times it can just go around them. It can erode rock over thousands of years, or it can carry tiny pebbles away.

In other words, water constantly changes shape and consistency, it's essential to survival and it chooses its own shape. Life is like that too. To control it, you have to master it and learn the source of its power and the nature of its course.

I like to think I'm like water that adapts to its surroundings and eventually finds a way in. It's certainly how I train, and how I've seen other great fighters evolve.

MASTER: *Every mixed martial artist will affirm that strength and conditioning is one of the cornerstones of conditioning. Georges shocks people when he tells them that strength and conditioning is probably the least important part of his workout, by far. If you look at the evolution of his strength and conditioning workout, it's not at all like so many young men of his generation with, basically, a bodybuilding workout. But as a young man, that's exactly what he would do: lift weights, do bench presses. Over the years, he went through more and more sophisticated approaches to conditioning. He's had a tremendous number of different workouts, different approaches. Each one was a significant improvement on the previous one.*

I didn't understand this before I changed my way of thinking, before I became interested in tactical and technical questions. I surfed on talent and physical ability. When I lost, I realized the status quo had to change. I realized I had no choice but to ask myself real questions. And the best question in the history of the world is also the simplest: Why and how did this happen?

MASTER: *And the study of gymnastics has brought Georges to a level of athleticism that is better than at any other point in his career.*

He was never just satisfied with hard work. Bodybuilding is hard work—you lift those weights and you feel exhausted—but it's not smart work. It's not going to make you a better athlete or a better mixed martial artist. And so Georges didn't just stay with the hard work; over a decade, he has constantly refined and rejected, moved on, rejected and moved on—until he found the apex of athleticism, which he believes is gymnastics. This is just one example where you see Georges working hard with a sense of vision.

When "normal" athletes do a backflip or a somersault, at the end of the move they see little stars against a black background for a fraction of second. Try it: do two or three cartwheels in a row. Blackout and stars, like when you stand up too quickly after lying down on the sofa for too long.

When gymnasts do much more complicated, intricate patterns on the mat or the rings, they don't see any stars. They just keep on spinning or leaping or twisting. They're so used to the motion that their head stays the same. Their stability is consistent throughout their exercises.

This is important if, like a gymnast, you're going to be doing ten consecutive somersaults. Flips and head-over-heels turns happen in mixed martial arts as well. So it's really important if you're going to fight Josh Koscheck, because you don't want to lose one one-hundredth of a second in the octagon against that guy. A split-second blackout is the difference between avoiding an overhand right and having it connect. The difference is winning and losing—it's as simple as that.

MASTER: *Too many people in mixed martial arts talk about hard work without intelligent hard work. It's the depth of insight that matters. What gives work an intelligent direction is what makes it useful. Georges is restless in his desire to find the most efficient use of that hard work. He's constantly looking for ways of improving his workout, constantly looking for new ways of applying rules to increase their efficiency rate. That is what makes him unique: his depth of insight and vision. Not just athletic ability and work ethic.*

I like to watch the best athletes in other sports and how they react or move in certain situations. It helps me understand my own movements better. I break down their processes, their reactions, their movements. They perform certain tactics at speeds that are far greater than my own. It is good to see them perform at these speeds, and to improve my ability to follow their progressions.

I've watched many champions, but Amir Khan, the great British pugilist, is my favorite, and his sparring is on another level. So fluid, he never, ever stands in front of his opponent. He always chooses an angle with which to confront his adversary. He seldom is ever hit by an inferior attack, and his counterattacking is simply sublime.

At home, I also watch former world champion wrestler Gia Sissaouri, an unbelievable athlete. He's so fluid and his combinations are so well organized and sequential, it's like choreography. He puts everything together seamlessly. When he attempts a single move, he's always ready for the counteraction. He's always ready to adapt, to move with the flow of power and use it to his own advantage. His incredible energy keeps him one step ahead of the opponent. The movement is so ingrained into his mind and body that it's subconscious. It's natural, a part of how Gia lives.

I like to watch Freddie Roach. Besides the fact that he's the best boxing coach in the world, in my opinion, I like the way he does what he does. I feel like I get better just being around him and listening to him coach his athletes.

I have often gone to Freddie Roach's gym and watched other people fight. Just walking into his gym feels special. You know, coming in, that it's about one thing in that place: boxing at the highest level. No cameras, no glitz, no bullshit. That's how a boxing club should be run.

Going to his gym is one of the rare times when I can actually sit still and just let my mind wander. Usually, I have trouble sitting around doing nothing. I'm just no good at it. I like to do two, three, four things at once. It drives some of the people around me nuts. Rodolphe is always trying to get me to stop texting or simply sit down. But I can't. I have to move. I can't stop myself. I'm addicted to movement and occupation of time and space. The only time I understand how it is for those without the same predisposition is when I'm around Freddie, because somehow, Freddie calms me down.

When I was recovering from my knee surgery in early 2012, I frequently went to visit his gym, the Wild Card, as often as I could. I didn't know what I was going to do at first, but Freddie told me, "Just come and we'll figure it out." He probably had a plan, because he always has a plan. He's that kind of guy—his vision and his understanding of things is completely unique. So I decided I was going to follow his advice and go visit him in his club.

"Sit there, and watch what they're doing," said Freddie, referring to the other fighters. "Watch their feet. Watch their hands and their hips and their heads and the movement they create. And learn from it."

So I decided to give it a try. Thank goodness I did. I discovered something amazing on the very first day: that I could learn from watching, not just doing.

My whole life has always been about building a knowledge base from doing—executing and repeating movements. Developing technique in a hands-on way. Feeling the evolution of movement with my own hands, and transmitting that to my brain so it could remember. But going to Freddie's gym showed me there are other, *different* ways to learn. It proved to me that the myelin sheath, which Rodolphe goes on and on about, works when it senses movements and not just when it executes them.

In fact, I think that watching others train helped me better understand technique and how to execute movements the right way. Many times, I felt like I was spying on two fighters who didn't know I was there, and taking their secrets with me.

Sometimes it would be a local guy working his way up, and other days it would be Amir Khan. Just watching these guys, these expert boxers, move and be fluid helped me improve my own technique. I'd watch them perform, and then I'd close my eyes and see myself moving better, punching more fluidly, absorbing blows more naturally, and it made me better. This technique is called *visualization,* and it turns out that it's quite detailed and specific.

Visualization is about imagining how something relates to your senses—feel, smell, taste and sound. It's not something you just decide to do by sitting there a few minutes—like all good things, it takes practice and an open mind. But when you do it right, your imagination makes it seem so real that it can trick your body into thinking it is reality. This is a very good thing.

How it works is pretty straightforward: you imagine good things happening in your mind, and you let them happen. After a while, they'll actually start happening in your life. For an athlete, this will be much more specific to performing an athletic feat, but it applies to all facets of life in my opinion, and you won't know or be able to judge it until you actually follow the rules and give it a try.

Using your own imagination to create mental images stimulates your mind, helps organize your life and keeps your focus in a particular direction. It allows your unconscious mind to work toward the image you have created, the goal. It's about understanding the life you want to live, and seeing it unfold before you.

Anyone who concretely visualizes a realistic and more immediate goal when planning for long-term success has a vastly better chance at change and achievement. When we realize the smaller successes, when the stepping stones are reached and become our new platform, we feel good about ourselves. We feel energized, like things are working right and we're making them happen. Eventually, this pushes us on to greater visions, greater goals, greater ambition. There is nothing more satisfying and more personally empowering than realizing a goal. This just puts a smile on my face.

It doesn't mean it's easy. How I adapt and change when confronted with something unexpected is important because life is unpredictable. Seeing tough situations as opportunities should be refreshing.

Again, no matter what is thrown into your path, with training and self-discipline, with clear focus and confidence, problems can be overcome and can even lead to unexpected gains. The edict "Learn one thing, learn one hundred thousand things," from the Japanese martial classic *Book of Five Rings* by Musashi Miyamoto, is perfect in this situation because it helps us to deal with the unexpected. This may not fall into the actual category of visualization, but perhaps by constantly practicing visualization, we can enhance our ability to think on our feet, to react in a calm, controlled way, no matter what happens.

It's important to visualize every fight, every opponent. You size him up, you look at him as objectively as possible, you look for real strengths and weaknesses, and if you're lucky, you discover the things your opponent wants to conceal. And then you keep going: you prepare your attack diligently, train to the utmost in the key techniques, select the right mode of attack. You visualize the fight and how you want it to go, seeing the defenses mounted in front of you, the attacks coming at you; all the while, you wait patiently for the hollow, the weak point, to develop. When you see it happen, the opening, you close in without revealing your intentions. When the time is right, you strike critically, decisively, with the confidence and power you've derived from constant training in body and mental awareness. Every step is visualized as realistically as possible.

Watching athletes who, in their own right, outperform me on many levels helps me improve my own visualization. It's never a bad idea to imitate the best of the best, or simply choose the best part of their lessons for your own benefit.

There are techniques for punches and kicks, but in my opinion they are only the beginning. Everybody is different, so the key isn't to force yourself to do the kick the way everybody else does it. The secret is in repeating the kick—or the punch—the best way you're able to do it, and then repeating it thousands of times. In the gym, in your own mind, at all times.

Do you watch too much TV? See yourself reading books tonight, the only thing to switch on being the lamp beside you. Eat too much fried food? See your lunch tomorrow full of healthy greens. Worried about that presentation and want to put it off? See yourself standing confident and knowledgeable in front of your audience, delivering and answering questions. It is no different from how I visualize myself, my opponent, the octagon and victory.

As you'll discover, Rodolphe is constantly talking to me about the brain's myelin sheath and its impact on my technique. To be honest with you, I don't really care what it's called; I care that it works. But if you ask Rodolphe, he'll explain it in relatively simple terms: the myelin sheath is a layer of matter around the axon of a neuron that helps increase the speed of brain impulses. It records movements. It's like an old vinyl record with layers of information layered into it—except that you can keep adding layers and improving the sharpness and crispness of the sound. Applied to sport, whether you're practicing a jump shot or a roundhouse kick, it works the same way: the more you repeat a movement exactly the same way as before, the better you become at mastering the movement. What happens, eventually, is that your body—thanks to your brain and the myelin sheath—

remembers exactly what needs to be done without you needing to remind it. Like a needle that plays a record, the song remains the same. Automatic.

I *reflect* on my movements. I replay them in my mind. I think about them—situations and scenarios. I believe that the brain needs this kind of practice and gets better even when I'm thinking of the move instead of doing it physically. It's perfect execution. I'm thinking about this stuff all the time. In fact, every day, I get lost in thought to the point that people talk to me and I'm not there. They have to snap me back into the present.

This is important because, as I enter tougher competitions against better opponents, I need my brain to focus on something other than performing movements. I need my mental focus to remain on strategy and decision-making, not technique and execution. Those must come naturally, because in a fight, there's no time to think about how to punch. There's barely enough time just to let the body do what the mind thinks is best.

MASTER: *The public perception of Georges is that of a mixed martial artist, certainly, but he sees himself as a martial artist, which is how I see him too. To differentiate, you must delve into a theory of what is mixed martial arts.*

People use the term martial artist *in an extremely loose fashion. The very idea of what is a martial artist has changed dramatically in the last fifteen years, with the advent of MMA. Many aspects of modern martial arts were not considered martial arts when I was a child. Wrestling, for example. Now, only a fool would deny that wrestling is a martial art. MMA, meanwhile, is a composite sport; it's a collection of other sports wedded together to form its basis. It's built out of freestyle wrestling, judo, karate, boxing, Muay Thai, Brazilian Jiu-Jitsu, sambo and various other combat sports.*

The only common feature of the various martial arts that form the basis of MMA is that they are all competitive sports. This is unlike the more eclectic styles of kung fu, for example, which have no sporting aspect, no competition of any kind.

And yet, MMA is something more than the sports that form its basis. The complex relationship between those component sports and the overall sport of MMA is a difficult one to describe. That's why mixed martial arts has always been a poorly understood phenomenon. I would go so far as saying that many of the athletes in the sport have a shallow understanding of the sport.

Before each one of my fights, I make a point of saluting my opponent. I salute the other fighter out of respect, even though he is trying to take something away from me. Not many people understand why I do this, but it's simple: without the other guy, there is no me. That's why I pray for the both of us, and not just myself. By stepping into the octagon, my adversary completes me. He makes my life possible. He becomes a part of my existence. To disrespect him is to disrespect myself. Thanks to him, I become a better man. Thanks to his presence, I am a true martial artist. Thanks to his willingness to face me, my life takes shape and moves forward, my path evolves and my life goal nears.

During the fight, my job is to win by fighting as little as possible. The greatest victories are those you don't even have to fight for. You just aim to reach the point when you can feel victory within your grasp. When do you know you've got the other guy beat? When he breaks down mentally. It's never truly over until it's over, but there is a breaking point when you know you've got him. When he is close to capitulation. When the end is near.

The reality and the danger, though, is that this is a dangerous time, perhaps the most dangerous for the fighter in the lead, in control. Because when your opponent is on his last hope, it means he's capable of trying anything. He's a desperate animal who will attack. He's a broken warrior whose last ounces of effort will be bunched into a final desperate lunge for a prayer, a flicker of hope, a miracle punch or kick.

But it's the last attack, usually.

Each fighter has a different "tell" for when he has broken down mentally. I've noticed that one great opponent of mine accepts dominance from his opponent when he leans against the cage to rest and, hopefully, regroup. I've observed another wiping the sweat from his brow with each hand, like a nervous tic. Many pull and grab at their own shorts repeatedly. Others just move differently and have a wild, foreign look in their eyes. It's always unique. It's often bizarre. And it can only be final.

Once it becomes final and the fight is ended, I bow to my opponent in praise and thanks. After the fight is a time for humility, acceptance and analysis, no matter the result. Sports are reality television, the best of it, but the "actors" are real people, real human beings who are walking the paths of their own lives. We can never forget that. Before the fight, you and your opponent are on opposing life paths. If he wins, he wakes up tomorrow and his entire existence has changed dramatically. When you're the champion, *if* you win, the next day is the same as it was yesterday. If you lose, *your* life has changed dramatically. This understanding extends to all things.

In one of my earliest fights, right after winning, it occurred to me to go see my fallen opponent, Justin Bruckmann, to make sure he was all right and congratulate him on his performance. He truly deserved it. After beating Pete Spratt, Pete and I went out on the town. After the referee's controversial decision against Ivan Menjivar, I took the mic and told the crowd that, despite the ruling, my opponent had not tapped out. I said that he wanted to keep going, and that we could keep fighting. They of course gave me the win, anyway, but I still consider that fight a draw. I was a long way from championship-caliber anything, but the truth comes out naturally when you live in balance. Human beings have a natural attraction to the truth, but winning can obscure the truth. One needs to remind oneself in victory *and* defeat.

After my fight against Koscheck, where I was painted the hero and he the villain, I felt compelled to quiet the crowd, telling everyone his prefight smack talk was just hype, just a way of getting fans involved. While it's important to build hype and get people excited about a fight, I know that bragging and threatening my opponent with destruction just doesn't fit my style. I come from the world of traditional martial arts, and that's something you just don't do. I know a lot of people would like me to say more, or do more before each fight, but I know myself, and I know what is (or *seems*) authentic and what is not. What I also know, though, is that prefight banter is good for some fighters— it helps them get ready, get psyched up. And some mixed martial arts fans love the controversy. The truth is, I kind of enjoy it myself when I'm not at the center of it. But when I am, it has served to motivate me.

But then there is a time to let go. There is a moment when you look at your opponent, and you must see yourself. Only then will you understand the words of one of my favorite quotes, which comes from St. Augustine: "Conquer yourself, and the world lies at your feet."

MASTER: *Georges had a very interesting sensei in his early years: Kristof Midoux. As a teenager, this sensei would literally make Georges fight grown men in all-out challenge matches. Georges, who had a very limited repertoire of grappling techniques, only knew a sloppy double-leg takedown* *and had his karate movement skills. And from those humble beginnings he was pushed into fights with grown men that could be wrestlers, boxers, karate specialists, et cetera. Georges would literally have to fight these men to the ground and, with his limited Brazilian Jiu-Jitsu skills, submit them. He had to shootbox them.*

I believe that if GSP had not met Kristof Midoux, he would not be the international success he is today. People often wrongly speculate on Georges's greatest influences, but I can tell you Kristof is one of the seminal favorites. Sometimes, from the craziest people comes a surprising wisdom.

There are moments during some fights when my mind wanders away from the octagon. Sometimes I've looked over at Dana White or Lorenzo Fertitta, the UFC bosses, and tried to read the expressions on their faces, tried to understand what's going through their minds. I remember very clearly looking out of the octagon once and locking eyes with Tito Ortiz.

I like Tito; he's a special kind of hero for me. It's because of martial artists like Tito, who paved the way for fighters like me, that mixed martial arts has come so far in our society. He's an old hand at MMA, the real deal of a man. Guys from Tito's generation made almost no money, had it tougher than anyone can imagine, and persevered for one reason: because they loved what they were doing. I admire those men. I understand their passion and I try to be respectful of it.

While I was holding an opponent against the fence, Tito and I looked at one another and I made a face at him, trying to express a thought—that what I was doing was going to be long and hard and tough. And he responded, just with his eyes and a slight movement of his head, like he was inside my thoughts and saying matter-of-factly, "Yeah, that's right. It's tough. Just get it done." I believed at that moment he really was inside my head because he'd been there before, in the ring. He had lived what I was living. He knew that in the octagon, nobody will fight for you. Nobody else will enter and do your job. When you're inside the octagon, the rest of the world is a distant place, without reach. There's you and there's your job, and over there is your opponent. Your job is to fight him and win.

MASTER: *In the early years, like any beginning student, Georges had some rough experiences. He was hit repeatedly. But as the mounting years went by, on an intuitive level, he started to integrate his karate movement patterns with the wrestling he was learning and the boxing he was beginning to pick up. As he embarked on his MMA career, you could already see the beginning elements of something truly great. His ability to cover distance, misrepresent his real intentions to his opponent and intimidate them with these great takedowns was interspersed with the threat of strikes. His ability to create his own rhythm while thwarting that of his opponent was there from those early days and, over time, was refined. In my personal opinion, it hit its apex the night Georges fought Josh Koscheck for the second time. I've watched him for well over a decade, doing his shootbox entry drills, and that night his shots were so fast I couldn't even see them coming. To his credit, Koscheck did a good job of getting back up. But the actual entries to the takedowns were as good as any human being will ever achieve. As a coach, that was one of the few times of my life that I looked upon a student in wonder.*

I rely on the power of the unexpected to defeat my opponent. The best example may be my takedown technique.

The secret is not in the *how,* it's in the *when.* Don't get me wrong: the *how* has to be near perfect, and it takes years to reach that point, but every good mixed martial artist can perform a takedown. When you're fighting against the best, the *when* is the secret.

I try to time my takedowns so they surprise my opponent. The best time to do that is to counter one of his attacks with a takedown. Think about it: when he throws a punch, the opponent doesn't expect me to come toward him. He thinks I'm going to move backward or sideways and avoid the punch or, at worst, block it. But I don't always do that. Sometimes, when I see the punch is coming because of a movement in his shoulder or the look in his eyes, I prepare for my own takedown. And when he throws that punch, before he has the time to hear the *poof!* of the air as his hand misses over my head, my shoulder is driving into his gut and I'm taking him straight onto the mat.

In one of my earliest professional fights against Spratt, very early on he went for a high push kick. The normal reaction you see is defensive, but I used the moment to spring at him and take him down. It wasn't a backward move, consciously trying to do things in reverse; it was a spontaneous reaction, plain and simple. I see openings and try to exploit them to my advantage. It was the last thing Pete—or, it seemed, anyone else—thought I would pull.

It's just the power of the unexpected.

MASTER: *One of the great features of Georges St-Pierre— and I'm absolutely certain it's one of the great reasons for his success—is the profundity of his thinking with regards to the complex relationship between the component sports of MMA and the sport of MMA itself. I taught Georges a*

component martial art—Brazilian Jiu-Jitsu and grappling.
He taught me the interface between the various component
martial arts. MMA is built up by the traditional combat
sports, but in unison, it somehow rises above the content of
those martial arts and becomes something quite different.
Georges had many coaches, all of whom taught him com-
ponent martial arts, but it was Georges himself who came
up with the interface between them. In so doing, he went
beyond the teachings of his masters.

That was another one of Bruce Lee's lessons: that no two
people are the same. This is important because it means that a
system that works for one person won't be perfect for another.
It means that individuality is a major part of expanding knowledge. Bruce called this aspect of training *totality*. He wanted people to become the most complete individuals possible. For me,
that has always meant one thing: to keep the knowledge that is
useful to me, and to let go the stuff that is useless. When I was in
college, I would work on karate one day, boxing the next, Brazilian Jiu-Jitsu the next, Muay Thai the next, trying out different
styles of fighting and filtering them for the most important, comfortable, useful elements. And even if Bruce Lee had been in the
room watching my training sessions, I am the only one who truly
knows what feels right versus what feels wrong, what I should
keep compared to what I should discard.

I see the world as a knowledge hardware store, and every day
I'm just walking through the aisles. All along the aisles they have
these knowledge keys. Each key opens a different door. When
I see or hear about something new that I like, I pick up the key
and open the door. If what's behind that door makes me better
at being who I really am, then I take it home with me. Once I

get home, I take that new knowledge to one of my three workshops, and I start working on it. The two basic workshops I have are a) the Physical Workshop and b) the Mental Workshop. So, for example, doing gymnastics goes in the Physical Workshop, while philosophical discussions about visualization, for example, go into the Mental Workshop.

The third workshop is the Fusion Workshop, where I put all that knowledge together in my own particular way. It's where shootbox comes from. It's what defines me best, to some.

> **MASTER:** *Shootbox has been perhaps the single most important ingredient in the development of Georges's success as a mixed martial artist. Shootbox is Georges's own term: it refers to the act of integrating striking skills with takedown skills. It is arguably the most important facet of MMA, because it gives the mixed martial artist the capacity to determine the direction of a fight. It enables a mixed martial artist to choose where the fight occurs, whether it occurs in the standing position, whether it is taken to the fence, whether it is taken to a clinch or whether it is taken to the ground. It enables you to take an opponent away from his strengths and toward his weaknesses. The man who determines the direction of a fight has a massive advantage in the context of mixed martial arts.*
>
> *Georges is without question the greatest shootboxer in the history of mixed martial arts. No one integrates the skills of kickboxing, the skills of takedown and punching, better than he does. When did this first occur to me? The first time I saw him fight. He was so far ahead of the game it wasn't even funny. Yet the development of shootbox is a long and complicated history, and it began long before I even knew who Georges St-Pierre was. No one ever even taught Georges to*

shootbox, and there's a simple reason: nobody teaches it. No one has the overall breadth of skills to be able to do so. They merely scratch the surface.

At any given time, in life or in battle, you only need to know two people to succeed: yourself and your opponent.

You are in constant change. Your weaknesses change shape. Sometimes they disappear. Your strengths grow, they evolve, and they too change shape. Power is different when you combine it with wisdom. Wisdom allows you to use less power to accomplish more tasks.

Your opponent, too, constantly changes. He changes shape. His nature, though, is always the same: he wishes to defeat you.

When I prepare for one of my fights, I want to be as far away from my opponent's thoughts as possible. I don't want him to see me, to feel me or even to think of me, wherever he is. I, on the other hand, think of him constantly. I keep him in my mind's eye and see him in every situation possible. I study him, how he moves, how he does battle, how he reacts. I try to reach an understanding of the best version of the truth on my opponent—to avoid the element of surprise.

The only way to eliminate the element of surprise is to know yourself *and* know your adversary. It's harder to know yourself than to know the enemy. Because when it comes to yourself, you have all these emotions—like pride, for example. You get carried away with your own emotions. In some of my fights, I lost control of myself, but if I'd known myself properly I would have calmed myself down immediately.

The truth is that I don't even want to make the opponent into an object of hatred. Hate isn't rational or intelligent. There's no point to it. Hate blinds individuals and removes reality from sight. There have been opponents whom I really didn't like, or who said things about me that really pissed me off, but that's just motivation. It's part of the game.

> **MASTER:** *You have to understand that shootbox somehow stands above its component parts. That is the key to understanding the greatness of Georges St-Pierre. Yes, he had good teachers, but all they taught him was components. What makes him great is not the components, it is the ability to go beyond those components into the sport of mixed martial arts itself (of which shootbox is one component—arguably the most important).*
>
> *GSP made a science of shootbox. That was not taught to him by any one person, that was self-taught. He invented it all on his own. And its development began out of simple necessity: self-defense.*

My front foot always points to my adversary. This is important because it stops my opponent from having or developing an angle on me. You can never allow that to happen because, quite simply, it exposes your blind side. It creates weakness. A fighter can't afford to leave his flank or his blind side open, ever.

Not addressing the opponent with your foot exerts a very negative influence on your power too. Misalignment reduces the power you can generate from one side of your body. So maybe you can throw a jab or a leg kick, but you make it very difficult to follow with a powerful combination from your strong side. In addition, you give the opponent more attack options while limiting your own angles and approaches.

Sometimes you can alter or play with the positioning of your feet as a feint, but it takes a master to succeed at this. Don't forget, you must first master the rules before you start breaking any of them.

My foot positioning, if I compare my first fight to my time as champion, is probably the biggest change in my style. In the beginning, I never paid attention to my foot positioning and seldom made sure my front foot pointed at my opponent. I didn't realize the importance of it.

Look at my legs, and the movement of my hands. Observe their position. When the fight begins, look at the way my foot points to my opponent, and my constant movement, and the way I move in and out of striking distance. See my hips and how fluid I try to keep them. And now look at my left hand, look at it dangling around by my hip, moving forward and back, swaying in time.

If it's difficult for you to see it, cue the Koscheck fight again. Do you see what I'm doing? It's the jab. It's all about the jab. Koscheck moves in and here's the jab, and I step back. Koscheck steps back in and jab after jab! And step back. Can you see it now? That's the way I fight.

And so now imagine I'm holding a foil in that hand. There's the handle and there's a blade at the end of it that hovers menacingly near my opponent. That's my stance, and it comes from fencing. I don't fight, I fence. That's not my fist, it's my foil. It's black, like my trunks, so you don't see it coming. It comes at you from a shadow. I am fencing.

The fencing idea I got from Bruce Lee, and he was talking about this a long time before I was even born. Most of my movement inside the ring is based on the fencing system. When I cut distance, it's the same movement as in fencing. I don't even have to take my right hand out, which is another thing Bruce Lee talked about. If you take the right hand out too much, you're off balance, which leaves you open to get hit. With the fencing approach you take fewer risks, you get hit less often, which is more important.

Look at Bernard Hopkins; he's still boxing at almost fifty years old. Nobody talks about his knockout power. But he's still in shape, he does what he likes, he's making money, and in his sport people appreciate what he's doing. They see the beauty and the grace in his approach. In MMA, there's still a chorus of people who complain that some fighters are not taking enough risks, but these individuals don't really know or appreciate the sport. They want contact, knockouts. But no sport, not even boxing, is solely about knockouts. In the ring, Hopkins beat Jean Pascal, the world champion at the time, and Hopkins was forty-six years old. Look at Andre Ward; he has consistently beaten people without ever knocking them out. Just try hitting him, just once. A knockout artist takes unnecessary risks, but, once he reaches a certain level, he's going to eat it from a real pro.

Look at Anderson Silva. His secret is his counterattack. Even when he's been close to defeat, it seems to me like he draws in his opponent and lets him think he'll win by KO, and then he submits with a surprisingly lethal hold.

Floyd Mayweather, same thing. He waits for the other guy to try and knock him out and seizes the opportunity. He lures you into his trap and finds ways of using your strength against you. I've seen Mayweather knock out a guy who was known as a knockout king, but he just waited for him. He waited patiently for the other guy to leave a opening, and then he pounced—like a fencer.

MASTER: *Georges began with karate, and he learned it in a very traditional sense. The great gift that karate gave him is the skill of movement. Movement and faking, the ability to interrupt his opponent's rhythm through the use of fakes and misdirection. That is what Georges took from karate. As he matured, he began to learn Muay Thai and boxing, and from* *these he learned how to hit high, and how to hold a stance, et cetera. And then began the study of freestyle wrestling, and he developed a very good proficiency in all of those.*

Now, most people learn a little boxing, they learn a little wrestling, they learn a little Muay Thai, and they haphazardly patch them together. Then they hope for the best when they get into a mixed martial arts competition. That's the extent of most people's development. But the possession of great credentials in any one of the martial art components guarantees nothing in your ability to shootbox, or your ability to punch your way into a takedown. You can be a great boxer, yet be afraid to throw a punch in a shootbox—because you're afraid of being taken down. You can be a great wrestler, but you can't score a single great takedown—because you're afraid of being punched in the face. And so on. Therefore, people can have what would appear to be outstanding credentials to make them a great shootboxer, and yet fail.

My own attack system is built around a code, a visual code that my mind has grown accustomed to. It starts in the fencing stance, and it evolves depending on the direction of the fight and the style of my opponent.

I've trained my mind to pick up key movements that make up the code for a jab, or a right-hand lead, or a kick or a takedown.

My system is designed to read the other guy's code; it's designed to counter any attack coming my way, which complicates things for all my opponents. So first, what the heck is a fighting code?

Well, it doesn't just exist in martial arts—it's about the origins of all movements and how our minds respond to seeing them. In baseball, for example, you can tell someone's going to swing the bat before the hands and arms even start moving to swing the bat—and that comes from looking at the hitter's hips, or sometimes his eyes. Or in poker, a skill game based on your cards, and your opponent: if you are good enough, you can tell when another person is bluffing you, or trapping you. All it takes is for your eye to catch someone's "tell," his or her code.

In any fighting art, a punch, kick or lunge has a beginning, a middle and an end. A jab, for example, starts on one side of the hips. So the code for a jab is a twitch in the hip.

When I watch my opponent, my mind automatically checks for all these signals, these codes, so that I can predict what's coming. Each one of his tactics is connected to a code. This is why preparation and practice are so crucial in the lead-up to a fight: you practice being able to tell what the other guy is planning on doing, because one thing is for sure: your mind is faster than any part of your body, and it controls your reflex time.

This is crucial to my style of fighting, because everything I do is built on speed: recognition and reaction. Many of my takedowns, for example, actually come when most other fighters would be moving backward to avoid contact. But when my mind catches a signal that your right-hand lead is coming, I have trained myself to be ready to pounce forward and avoid contact. I dip my head to avoid the punch, I move my hand upward to ensure there's no contact or damage, I dip my shoulder into your mid-waist area, and I try to take you down as fast as possible to gain an advantage and position.

In recent years, I've worked on new kinds of strikes to fool everybody's fighting code. I was in the gym one day and this guy who comes to Tristar was being laughed at because of the way he was throwing his jab. Instead of just extending his arm forward in a straight line, the way a jab is usually thrown, he was extending his forearm upward across his face so that it would fall on the other guy's face or forehead. It looked like he was trying to hit the top of the other guy's head.

It seems weird and awkward, but I decided to try anyway and see for myself. It's a good thing I did, because I learned something: the mind isn't used to seeing a punch come from that direction, which means that very few fighters' codes are prepared for what I now call the Looping Jab. It's not a knockout punch by any means, but I've landed it many, many times, and that's important in a professional fight, if just for the element of surprise.

It all begins with training at very slow speeds. If you ever get a chance to visit Tristar Gym when I'm training, you can see me in the ring, boxing almost in slow motion without gloves on. My practice partner and I are taking turns throwing different punching and kicking combinations so we can recognize the code—we need to give our powerful brains the time to get used to the code. As we get warmer and better, and as our brains start developing better reaction times, we gradually speed up into full sparring mode.

Every single person has a code, a way to throw a punch or a kick, and every single human being should be able to develop a code, a warning system based on experience. It's why people brace themselves when they're about to get hit with a water balloon, for example, or why they hesitate to jump into a lake: their brains are telling them they're about to get wet, and it could be really cold. The brain, and therefore the body, prepares them for what's coming. The same is true in fighting at all levels—it's just that professionals have more advanced systems. It's only natural, because that's what we do for a living. More importantly, it doesn't just work on defense.

I'm not naive enough to think that I'm the only fighter in mixed martial arts who's practiced at catching codes—we all are training this way. At this level, it becomes a game of skill by the best in the world.

MASTER: *I'd seen Georges fight on tape, but the first time I saw him fight live was when he asked me to corner him for his first fight against B.J. Penn. At that time, Penn was correctly regarded as the number one pound-for-pound fighter in the world. He had gone up a weight division and defeated Matt Hughes. He was a world champion in Brazilian Jiu-Jitsu, just an extraordinary talent.*

I'd asked for John's advice on fighting B.J. Penn, and he offered to help me: the next day at six o'clock.

"Six p.m.?" I hesitated.

"No. Six a.m. My place."

Despite the hour, I went. It was the opportunity I'd been looking for, so I jumped.

MASTER: *When Georges was named as [Penn's] opponent, most people assumed that if the fight went to the ground, Georges was essentially done for. Georges at that time was fairly average on the ground, and Penn had some excellent Brazilian Jiu-Jitsu in some areas (but quite limited skills in others).*

I got to John's place, on time, despite another late night, and followed him inside. I sat down, and he immediately began speaking, delivering a blow-by-blow, full analysis of my opponent. He went straight to my weakness, and then presented a step-by-step guide based on the things he'd seen from B.J. Penn, covering every angle possible, from start to finish.

MASTER: *Now, everyone knew that B.J. Penn was extremely dangerous with his Brazilian Jiu-Jitsu when he was on top of his opponent. But I believed that he was not a dangerous fighter from underneath, and my reasons were simple:*

Penn had never submitted anyone from underneath. His strength was the ability to control people on top, pass their legs (their guard) and get into ground-and-pound position. That's where he's most dangerous, and if he had gotten into that position against Georges, he probably would have won. I, however, did not see him distinguished at all from the bottom position. I was confident that if Georges was able to get a fix on Penn's limitations, he could win decisively.

Against everyone's advice, I advocated a strategy that Georges push Penn back to the fence, put him down on his back, and ultimately win by the accumulations of rounds through ground and pound. After all, one of Georges's greatest strengths is his ability to put people down and control them on the ground, as well as to avoid submission holds and enact a ferocious ground-and-pound attack. I saw that as a happy marriage between Georges's best skills and B.J.'s weaknesses.

Now, I was the new guy in his corner and he had an established crew from Montreal. They thought I was out of my fucking mind, and they told me so. I understand why they thought that way because, on the surface, why would you take a champion known for his ground game to the ground? I just saw things differently. The real question, to me, was "Where is he good on the ground?" Don't give me generalities. Be specific! Specifically, Penn's very good on top. Extremely dangerous if he gets on your back. But he's not dangerous coming from underneath. Never was. Never has been.

Sometimes you need someone from the outside to take a good look at you and tell you the truth. Tell you what's really happening. Sometimes you don't realize what kind of person you are; you need that external feedback. It's not enough to just look in the mirror; you need someone to tell you 'You're doing this" or "You're doing that." People think the adversary is the tough part.

A friend of mine who loves jazz recommended a documentary he saw on John Coltrane, the legendary saxophone player. Coltrane was a machine, apparently. He would play a club date and then go to his hotel room and keep rehearsing, sometimes all night, alone. He just kept going, seeking perfection. While I'm more of a hip-hop guy, I learned something very important from Coltrane and how he handled his entourage.

One day, Coltrane was in the studio, recording some tracks, and some friends were hanging around, listening. Coltrane was improvising a solo and struggling to find the emotion, the effect he was aiming for. After playing the same song for the third time, one of the friends listening spoke up and said the version he had just played was really good, that she loved it.

Coltrane responded, "What was different about it that you liked?" But she couldn't answer. She just said she liked it, but couldn't define a specific or particular reason. She was probably tired of hearing the same tune three times in a row and was covering for it. So Coltrane asked that the next time she have a reason for liking or disliking something, because if she doesn't have anything to back it up, the feedback was useless.

He was doing for her what he expected from her: honesty. Honesty so that it leads to improvement. I don't know much about jazz, but Coltrane made sense to me that day.

MASTER: *"No, that's crazy—we're going to win on the feet," the others said in response to my strategy. But Penn is an extraordinarily gifted boxer, and his style of counterpunching was very badly matched versus Georges who, at that stage of his career, had a rather naive, straight-punching left-right* *combo. I really wasn't confident that Georges could win in a boxing exchange against Penn. Of course, I was the new guy and didn't want to appear disrespectful, so I responded: "How about we use your strategy for the first round, and if it works, we'll keep going with it? If it doesn't work, we'll switch to my strategy." They agreed. Now, as history recalls, Georges took a terrible shellacking in that first round. He got poked very severely in the eye early in the fight, and his straight style of punching was easily countered with Penn's jabs and counterpunching.*

When Georges came back into the corner at the end of that first round, he looked like a completely beaten man. He sat down for a short time of rest. Somewhere in that minute he found his strength and I looked at him. I said, "Georges, you know what you have to do." He turned his head up and looked straight at me. I remember he wiped the blood off his face and he nodded. He didn't say a word. He rose, and he immediately drove B.J. Penn to the fence, right there in front of me. We called out the precise elements we had drilled in New York City—based on risk control and dropping to a leg—and famously Georges took B.J. down on several occasions. Of course, he easily survived on the ground and Penn never got close to a submission. Georges dominated the next two rounds and won a narrow decision.

If we had used my strategy from the start, it would have been an easy victory, 3–0. But I learned a lot about Georges in that fight, something that went far beyond the technical level and into his heart. Even with that terrible start, he still came through, two rounds to one. He showed impressive courage, and I got to see his shootbox skills firsthand against, at that time, one of the greatest martial artists in the world.

It was surprising to the naive, but to those who under-stand strategy and B.J. Penn, there was nothing surprising about it. It was simply the observation of what should have been obvious facts. But most people overlook obvious facts.

World champions need "truth-sayers" around them, and John Danaher is a truth-sayer. A truth-sayer is a person who doesn't bullshit you about everything. A truth-sayer is someone who has enough respect for you to tell you the truth and help you differentiate the real from the mirage. That's one of the reasons I'm also so close to Firas, who became my full-time coach after my loss to Serra. One of the things we immediately agreed on is that the truth rules and takes priority over everything else. It's one of the reasons that Firas has become one of the world's greatest mixed martial arts coaches and that his gym, Tristar, is ranked with the best ever. In fact, we've never lost a fight together. But the most important reason Firas is my head coach is that he only knows to speak the truth, and I need that.

There's an entire collection of mirages waiting for you when you become a world champion for the first time. Obviously, you wake up the day after winning and you have only friends left in the world. Everybody likes you (except maybe the guy you beat last night) and wants to help. Everybody wants to be there and play a role and give you tips, et cetera. And if you believe all of them (including the voice inside your head that reminds you how great you are), you start believing that you don't need to train as hard anymore, that you've earned the right to party and be cool, that you can get away with taking it easy and not preparing as much for the next fight.

As champion, I had everyone around me—in the gym, on the street, in interviews, wherever—telling me I was the best, I was so great, I was this, I was that. The impact was not good because it only catered to my ego, which created an imaginary place. I put myself inside this beautiful, *imaginary* place where I was separated from all the other fighters by a line—a line that nobody else could cross. It was my place alone. But all of this just created a big illusion. Illusions are temporary. You're the same person after you become world champion as you were before you were world champion. Even the belt, other than looking good on the wall, has no uses. It doesn't even hold up your pants.

Then again, it isn't much better when you lose. When you're still the title holder, people say you're a great Quebecer, a fantastic fighter, and you represent all these great, wonderful, beautiful, perfect, gorgeous things. After my loss to Matt Serra, I realized it's the opposite. The road back down to reality is slick. You don't get to choose when the slide ends. You don't get to decide where it stops. You go down on your backside. There are no stop signs on this road, there's only rock bottom. People start saying things like, "He wasn't that good. We knew it all along. It was all luck." Both positions are extreme, and both are fundamentally wrong. You're always the same person, and you're always just trying to get better at something.

What it means to me is that truth-sayers hold the key. Opinions from people whose emotions matter more than facts are flawed. They aren't what you need if you want to become greater at something. What you need is competing evidence, a reason to keep striving for even greater things. Telling a person what they want to hear instead of what they need to hear is not really a winning combination.

I believe that real friends are truth-sayers. They'll tell you when you're full of crap, or when you're being lazy, or when you're being rude, or when your ass looks fat in those jeans . . .

MASTER: *Whether or not I had ever met Georges St-Pierre, my life would be unchanged: I wake up, I teach Brazilian Jiu-Jitsu all day, and I come home at night. Certain aspects of my knowledge base would be deficient, but the living of my daily life would be the same. I have a belief that all human greatness is founded upon routine, that truly great human behavior is impossible without this central part of your life being set up and governed by routine. All greatness comes out of an investment in time and the perfection of skills that render you great. And so, show me almost any truly great person in the world who exhibits some kind of extraordinary skills, and I'll show you a person whose life is governed largely by routine.*

That's why we get along—because John and I are both obsessively compulsive. We will spend hours repeating a single technique, over and over again until I get it right. We will repeat the move. We will sit and discuss it, then start over again. We will block out all other things. We will restart until the world dissolves completely. Until nothing else matters or even exists. We will repeat it until it is mastered, no matter when that will be. One certainty, though: it *will* be.

MASTER: *What we have in common is that we are both perfectionists. That explains some of our greatest strengths and some of our greatest weaknesses. I'm a stickler for perfection and the application of technique, and sometimes my criticisms can be somewhat harsh. Yet, many was the time that I would show a class a technique, and then I would go away and teach other classes back to back. I would look over at the far side of the academy and see Georges, still working that same technique, having gone through six or seven training*

partners because no one else could keep up with the intensity
of his own training.

It's like chewing a bite a hundred times to make sure you taste every single morsel of food: it makes things easier to process. And now I know: this is how I get better. I pick small things and I practice them until they're perfect.

I have no choice, because there are two kinds of people who do martial arts: those who practice a thousand different kicks one time each, and those who practice one kick a thousand times minimum.

You can guess which group I belong to.

MASTER: *As cold as I am to the average person, I'm warm to the exceptional and the gifted. It's natural, of course, that because Georges has become such a talented person, I should warm to him. But there's more to it than that. Even for someone as cold-hearted as I, I recognize in him attributes it would take a colder heart than mine not to be impressed by. He's extremely generous, he's an extremely giving person, in some ways shockingly naive. He's got this small-town charm that's difficult to deny. He's a genuinely good person who means well. Georges could, with his martial skills, be an absolute killer, but he's not. He's a consummate gentleman.*

The juxtaposition between his martial skills and the warmth of his character is impressive when you know him. It exhibits one of the great points that lies at the fundamental structure of all martial arts: control. Without controlling the most chaotic situation of all, which is a fight between two human beings, all control of other people begins with self-control. Georges is this guy with these tremendous martial skills, but he'd never use them in any context other than a professional fight (or if it was entirely appropriate to use them). And so he exhibits tremendous control over the skills that he has; that, I think, is the quintessential expression of what it is to be a martial artist.

But I'm not perfect.

I remember one time when I was fighting at the Bell Centre in Montreal. As I was walking toward the octagon, I took a look at the crowd. I have a good visual memory and can replay many of my fights and remember them blow by blow. But what happens right before a fight is often a blur. During my walk out, I rarely ever register the faces of the people or recognize who's there because I'm so focused on what's about to happen.

On this occasion, I remember looking into the stands and seeing a face I recognized, and he was wearing sunglasses. I remember thinking: *Why the heck is that guy wearing sunglasses indoors? That's weird. I think I know him. Oh, that's Luc Plamondon, the Quebec music star! Why is Luc Plamondon at my fight? And why is he wearing sunglasses? That's weird.*

What is really weird is that I clearly remember stopping and thinking all these things until I stopped myself and came back into the present.

Holy crap, I have to fight in three minutes. I need to wake up.

And so I turned away from him and went on my way, and luckily regained my focus and won the fight.

But that's not the dumbest example of how my mind wanders at the worst of times. During one of my championship bouts, and I won't tell you which one because the other fighter may be offended, I totally lost my focus in the middle of the action.

I remember it was a very tactical fight, not a swing fest. I was standing over the challenger and had him wrapped up against the fence in a defensive position. Sometimes it can take many seconds to get your opponent in the best place for a submission hold or an all-out attack. Anyway, I remember that he was leaning against the fence and I was standing over him, and my eyes wandered into the stands—which, with arms and legs flying, is never a good idea. I noticed these beautiful long locks of brown hair attached to an extremely beautiful and sexy woman. I couldn't take my eyes off her, especially when I realized it was Cindy Crawford.

Holy crap, I thought, *that's Cindy Crawford, and man, she looks amazing.* I kept staring at her until I caught sight of the man sitting in the seat next to her. He wasn't as good-looking as her, and he certainly had noticed how I was looking at his girl. I thought: *Holy crap, Cindy Crawford's husband looks pissed off at me! He came here to see me fight, and here I am checking out his girl. I have to stop this.*

So I took one last good look at Cindy, because she's so pretty, and then I went back to work. And I won again. Sure, it was risky and dumb, but I don't think I had a choice. If you don't believe me, you've never stared into Cindy Crawford's eyes when she's just a few feet away from you.

MASTER: *On the face of it, Georges shouldn't be a successful person at all. He was never an outstanding student in school. At the time I met him, he was working odd jobs and didn't really seem to have much going for him. And yet now he's a recognized guy with millions of fans and is by all accounts extremely successful. This is largely because he had a tremendous sense of vision, he had an extremely clear idea of what he wanted to do and where he wanted to do it.*

Many people have a good idea of what they want to do in their lives, but they lack the discipline and the patience to work their way there. What anyone, regardless of whether or not they're interested in martial arts, can take away from the story of GSP is the power of the marriage of vision with discipline. The combination of those two can yield tremendous results. The secret is routine. There's nothing more chaotic than a fight between two human beings. Who wins and who loses, even with trained athletes, is never certain. Show me the greatest mixed martial artist in the world, and there's always a chance he'll get knocked out by an also-ran. In the case of two untrained people fighting, it's just wild chaos, and usually the more aggressive (or bigger) guy wins.

The greatest lesson I have imparted to Georges has been to approach life with the outlook of probabilism. We live in a world of uncertainty. In a world of uncertainty, the best a man can do is stack the odds in his favor. To a certain degree, we are all subject to luck, circumstance, chance or fortune . . . call it what you will. Where there is no certainty, we must strive to create a set of conditions where we raise the probability to the greatest degree possible of bringing about a set of circumstances we want. Nowhere is this more true than in Georges's life, than in the world of fighting.

Outside the octagon, Georges is a complete gentleman. Inside the octagon, he's a chess player. Great fighters find ways to be great that are often quite different. Some of them are destroyers, like Mike Tyson, who go in to intimidate and crush. Others are artists, like an Anderson Silva, who seem to float in an ethereal way and somehow, without appearing to be trying, achieve a spectacular victory. Georges is more of a scientist: a cold, rational thinker, bouncing probabilities, looking for ways to subvert his opponent's attacks before he begins them. Maximizing the likelihood of his own success while minimizing the likelihood of his opponent's.

The key is to use the other person's power. It's like a chess game. You study each other, and you pick your points, his weak spots and how you think you can exploit them. Here's an example of the way I fight professionally, especially when the other guy is the challenger: I start with trying to win a small exchange, maybe two. I want to score some points. After a couple of rounds, though, I'm hoping that, like in a chess game, I'm ahead by a few pawns. When this happens, the opponent, if he has a chance at all, will have to open up somewhat. He'll be forced to take risks. That's how the game works—when you're the champion and you're ahead on points, you don't have to take risks. The other guy does, especially because he wants your title. He has to come and get it. And what usually happens when a fighter falls behind on points to a champion is that he opens up at the wrong time and eats it really good. Guys like Mayweather and Hopkins, they've understood that. Sugar Ray Leonard used his head the same way; he rarely took risks and won a lot of fights.

Against Koscheck, I relied on my jab to build my lead, and I expected him to open up. It wasn't my risk to take, it was his, and he, wisely, wasn't willing to take it. I wouldn't have either, and I didn't. You can call it boring if you like, for me it's a victory. If I'm behind, I'll take the risk, but you'll have to get me there.

In my first fights—against Karo Parisyan, for example—I didn't have a choice. I had to take chances and go all out. I constantly exposed myself to danger. That's what it is when you're just starting out.

But I've changed a lot as a fighter since then. I try to get hit as little as possible. I aim to bring my opponent toward me so I can decide when to attack, or counterattack one of his weaknesses. I use the fencing stance to keep my measure from his lethal strikes and to set up my own attack.

MASTER: *And so the question arises: How will you control chaos? Why is it that when Georges St-Pierre is 22–2, most mixed martial artists are 10–10? Why are Georges and Anderson Silva nearly undefeated? What is different about these guys? How do they control such a chaotic situation? What I always advocated in my teaching of Georges is the high-percentage approach. Minimize the risk while maximizing the risk to your opponent.*

A lot of people have criticized me for the fight against Koscheck. They were disappointed because they wanted to see a knockout, they wanted me to go for it. Well, I didn't "go for the knockout" against Koscheck, and there's a reason for it: I didn't need to. He didn't go for it against me either, and he probably should have because he trailed for most of that fight. I started that fight with the jab and it helped me build a lead. Then I stuck with the jab and it helped keep Koscheck at a distance, it kept him honest. My jab worked so well that he and I both knew he'd have to take a big risk to get around it. In our sport, at our level, risk equals knockout, and not usually for the guy ahead in the fight. When you take a risk against me or Koscheck, the chances are you're the one who'll get knocked out. When people start understanding the science of mixed martial arts better, they'll also understand this part of the fight game. In boxing, for example, when you look at a Hopkins or a Mayweather, you don't complain when one of them wins a "scientific" battle. One day, that will be true too in MMA.

As for me, even if my early fights weren't studies in science, I knew instinctively that I had to showcase different styles and approaches to be successful. As a young fighter, I was already experimenting with a sudden, unpredictable (but for me logical) mix of styles. Against Spratt, for example, I made sure he couldn't kick me and I took him to the ground, something everyone told me to avoid. Against Jay Hieron, I was using the ground-and-pound, and when he thought he had a handle on my game plan, I hit him with an unexpected right, out of the mixed karate and boxing method. And for my first fight against Hughes, I went for an early takedown and got him on his back. I was far from a finished product by any means, and even further from legitimate championship material, but I knew my opponents and picked up on surprising elements from a mix of styles to confuse and defeat them.

The key for me was to understand the use of all fighting stances. Fighting stances meet and are connected by an invisible thread. Your brain is the one that controls the thread and makes strategic choices. Broken down simply, here's how my brain works it: take a boxer to the ground, keep a wrestler on his feet, and *never waste energy in transition to try and bring someone to ground*—it's too tiring. Think about it. A specialist will use a lot of energy to bring you to his strength. Tactically, you have to manage this so that, even if you don't end up in his strength area, his energy reserves are depleted compared to yours. I often let guys out of a hold because I don't want to waste energy trying to keep them down while they just sit there, breathing, resting and thinking.

On top of that, as I've already said, I'm not the kind of fighter who gets hit a lot. Sure, I take some shots and I've been hurt, but I try to be as fluid as possible. One of my qualities is that I rarely get hit hard. I'm good at that. It's very tactical and based on patience. I'd rather pick my spot than take one shot so I can try to deliver five in return. My body is my working tool and I don't want to harm it, if possible. My favorite fighters are guys like Hopkins, who's still fighting in his forties because he was able to control the big hits he took and minimize their long-term impact. He can roll with the punches. It's all about absorption and constantly moving and staying out of the striking axis. Simply getting out of the way. Sometimes you take a shot, but not a direct shot. Roll, be fluid and never stay right in front of your opponent.

> **MASTER:** *Georges is a man of two worlds. He has learned (and continues to learn) martial arts as a traditionalist—the martial art of wrestling, the martial art of Brazilian Jiu-Jitsu, Muay Thai, et cetera. But more importantly, he transcended those arts when he became a mixed martial artist. That's where he became inventive, creative, that's where he stepped beyond the influence of his masters and became a master himself. He became a master of something that none of his masters were familiar with. Georges is one of the most inventive and creative people I have ever met.*
>
> *When you analyze Georges as a martial artist, you must consider his world view. At the deepest level, his world view is steeped in the idea of evolutionary theory. That's why he's obsessed with the study of ancient life forms, with paleontology. He's fascinated by who made the grade and who died out. He sees life in Darwinian terms: everything is a struggle for limited resources. All life is competition, in other words. And there's no more perfect metaphor for competition than the life of a fighter. It is a competition for a very limited resource: a championship belt. The competition is intense and Darwinian in the extreme. You have to keep evolving, moving forward.*

I have a friend who once told me that he doesn't like scary movies, and I asked why. His answer: *because they're scary.*

Makes sense. He doesn't invite fear into his imagination and thus his life. I try to do the same thing because, quite frankly,

I have an active enough imagination—it doesn't need someone else's imagination activating new *illusory* fears. Fear and the people who promote it drain my energy.

This all sounds so simple, but the point that needs to be made here is about who we let into our inner circles and the environment we create for ourselves.

Right before my first championship fight against Matt Hughes, the atmosphere was unbelievably dreary. People looked at me like it was the last time they were going to see me, like I was off to major surgery or about to go to war. And then, to make it worse, I'd turn on the television and catch footage of Matt Hughes on different channels. It seemed like he was everywhere. Like all the channels were showing the great Matt Hughes, my idol, slamming people into the ground. I was already scared as hell, and everyone around me with their words of "consolation" made it worse. Then they'd see Hughes walk by, and they'd point and whisper loudly: "There he is, there's Hughes! There's the champ!"

My dad leaned in close and, with a "comforting" hand on my shoulder, looked into my eyes and whispered, "It'll be okay."

In short, we weren't quite ready to fight for the belt, but I learned that I had to better control my own circumstances before a big fight.

On the days leading up to a fight, I need to be around other fighters, other people who understand what I do for a living. Because around them I get to feeling normal, and I need that because of what my mind is about to ask my body to do. Fight days are especially odd days. You feel a bit weird, and the air seems to feel different, like it knows what's about to happen. It must be all the energy, the conflict, the expectation. Yes, the chaos. Every movement feels so serious, and heavy.

MASTER: *Georges's deepest aim is to be considered the greatest martial artist of all time. That's a lofty goal and I'm glad he's got it, but it's also a very difficult one. It becomes very subjective, especially when you go outside your weight class, of which I've never been a fan. The most concrete goal is to be the best in your category. There is no talk, only action. You fight the people for real. There's no, "This guy was bigger, this guy was smaller."*

One of the things I've learned in my career is that our minds pick up all kinds of information that our consciousness never tells us about. We have to train ourselves to recognize and process this information because it's vital.

Here's an example: I was sparring with a guy who was shorter than me but had a really long reach. I didn't see this right away, but when we were sparring I kept getting hit by his jab and I started having doubts about my own efficacy and defensive skills. I realized a bit later, though, when we were shaking hands, that he had a really long reach. My mind didn't pick this up right away, which is why I was standing too close to him in the ring, which explains how he kept connecting with my face. My mind had processed his height but had underestimated his reach.

The lesson is this: there is something to be learned from shaking hands with your opponent, and that is his reach. You never base your distance on height exclusively, but on reach too. The last thing you want is a guy with a longer sword . . .

MASTER: *I am just a Brazilian Jiu-Jitsu coach, but I don't want Georges to go on fighting forever. Fighting, for Georges, is a difficult thing. Most of the people that I coach, they love to fight. Georges loves to train, but he doesn't love to fight.*

Fighting is stressful and difficult for him. It's not something he enjoys. He doesn't enjoy walking into the octagon and fighting another man. Other people I coach, you have to hold them back because they're so hungry to get in front of a crowd and exhibit their skills. Georges was never like that, not from the beginning and not now. For him to step out there is an emotionally wrenching thing to do. To see him fight at forty-five would be inappropriate. He'll need a viable career change.

I think if Georges could live his lifestyle without fighting, he'd choose that. As it goes now, he has to fight. That doesn't make the fighting any easier to do. It detracts from it—it's hard. Just the act of going out there. He's a Canadian figure and he carries the hopes of Canada. It's a lot to carry on a young man's shoulders.

In MMA, the crowd is unbearably fickle. You have two losses in a row and you're a has-been and a nobody and all your wins before were just dumb luck. It's a brutal, brutal world. It's Darwinian as they come. It's a world of evolutionary thuggery. Would you want to do that forever? Would you find it enjoyable? I don't know . . .

Losing really stinks when it happens in the octagon. Because it happens in front of thousands of screaming people, in an arena under the glare of lights and HD cameras that capture every angle, while millions of MMA fans are watching at home and in bars. This includes family, friends, coaches and training partners, and it feels like I'm letting all of them down. It's horrible, it's embarrassing, it's shameful, and, to make things worse, it *physically* hurts. It's bizarre: a punch in the face hurts less when you win than when you lose.

I also see the impact that losing has now on all my fans. I read about it and hear about it from them directly. Some of my fans spend thousands of dollars to fly to one of my fights, and I hate letting them down. I hate it.

Losing only becomes tolerable when you can look at it objectively and find ways of learning from it. So liking to lose happens later, much later, when I'm sitting alone in a room, going over every single step of what exactly happened and why. Losing is good when I am able to dissect the reasons why, which opens the way to finding solutions. This is when things get interesting.

Just after I tore my ACL in December 2011, the UFC title was awarded on an interim basis to Carlos Condit after his win against Diaz. Carlos had earned it. I lost more than the undisputed title, though. I lost a lot of money, for some reason I lost some friends, and I probably lost some fans too. But I gained a lot more than I lost. I gained knowledge—about me *and* about the world and the people close to me. Which brings me to the subject of Pyrrhic victories.

A Pyrrhic victory is a win that costs the victor so much, that to win this way again will cause a great defeat. The expression comes from around the third century B.C., in "honor" of an army that beat the Romans, but cost the king most of his men. One more victory like this, King Pyrrhus of Epirus said, "and I'll come home alone."

What it means is that you have to calculate the cost of victory every single time you enter battle—whether it's in the octagon or in everyday life. The easiest example is an argument with your girlfriend: sometimes you want to be right so bad, you'll say anything to win the argument. But is it worth the cost if you hurt the other person's feelings? If she leaves you because of a stupid argument?

I much prefer Pyrrhic losses, I guess, if such a "reversal" is even possible. You lose, but you learn so much that, eventually, you gain. I believe that our greatest victories in life are hidden behind our biggest losses. In my first fight against Matt Hughes, I was intimidated—I couldn't look him in the eye. I lost with a single tick left in the first round. Truthfully, I'd been defeated much earlier than that.

* * *

One day while cutting weight, I walked into the sauna for a sweat, and there, miraculously, was Hughes. "Hello, Georges," he said in his deep, powerful voice. He really freaked me out. I could hardly say hi, let alone engage him in conversation. So I just took a seat. Not long after, I couldn't take the heat anymore and I stepped out of the sauna. My guys were waiting outside with their credit cards and began scraping the sweat off my body, thinking it would help me lose more weight. We were actually trying to get more water out of my pores, and we thought little plastic cards would help. It was an organizational nightmare. We didn't know anything. Hughes was watching us and probably laughing at the rookies we were.

It was so early in my career. I'd been an undercard (so to speak) for a few fights, and suddenly, here I was in the championship. With sweaty credit cards and salty lunches.

* * *

I've changed since that fight. I've learned to treat fighters equally, with respect, but not hold them above me. There was a point in the first Hughes fight when I realized I could beat him. We were in a clinch and I was controlling him and the rhythm of both our movements and I remember thinking, *Wow, this is Matt Hughes and I'm in control and it wasn't too hard, and I know now that he can be defeated.* I didn't win that time, but I came out knowing I could, one day, with effort and strategy.

> **MASTER:** *What can the average person learn from Georges to benefit their lives here and now? On the face of it, it's absurd to wonder how a guy who works 9-to-5 in a bank can learn from a guy who lives such an extreme lifestyle as Georges's— a lifestyle of preparation for war and fighting a trained killer in a cage, in front of millions of people. These are different worlds. Georges wakes up at 11 a.m. every morning and trains for eight hours, then sleeps at 2 a.m. every day. He lives in a strange, alien world that has no relationship whatsoever to the average person.*
>
> *But always remember one thing: long before he was GSP, he was just plain old Georges St-Pierre. He was that lonely kid who spoke no English, coming on a bus away from Montreal. That is where you see the seed of greatness.*

The line between champion and runner-up is an odd thing. I didn't see it right away the first time I crossed it. I didn't understand what it meant. I only started truly knowing where and *what* the line is after losing my title the first time. I saw it on the way back down, and I realized that the line is intangible— you can't hang on to it, ever. Because life is not a straight line— it's in constant movement, and it chooses to be transparent when *it* wants to, not when you want it to be.

Age plays a factor in everything. Good genetics is helpful, of course, but talent is often overevaluated. Most champions started in their sport very young—whether in karate, wrestling, tennis or another sport—and they had the rare discipline to focus on no more than a couple of sports that intersect, like karate and wrestling, or soccer and basketball, or even rowing and kayaking.

I also often see little brothers and little sisters do well because they spent years having to (and badly wanting to) catch up to their older siblings and their friends. When you're someone's younger sibling, you often find yourself chasing after their dreams, being picked last, playing against older, stronger kids—all of which is good for you in the long run. From a young age, little brothers and sisters start at a disadvantage: they have to improve and constantly chase others, and they understand immediately what motivation means. All that because they seek acceptance. They must.

Another important element in becoming a champion is entirely related to luck. I call it "champion's luck," and it's all about timing. Granted, I created many of my opportunities, but they would have meant very little if I hadn't met the right people at the right time.

Then, of course, there's the element you can control, and that's work ethic. Rodolphe has a great quote: "Genius is one-tenth inspiration and nine-tenths perspiration."

MASTER: *Even then, in his broken English, he talked to me about becoming UFC champion. He was clear as day. He literally, when he looked in the mirror, saw a future champion. He had the will and the patience to give himself time to do what it takes. That's not an empty dream.*

Another integral ingredient to being a champion is *belief.* But you need two kinds of belief. You need belief that you can make it, so you carry confidence with you everywhere you go. And you need disbelief and disbelievers, people who don't think you can make it. Those people are incredibly important because they're the ones who inspire you to do the work, even when you don't feel like it.

The disbelievers are everywhere; some are good to you, while others are bad because they're jealous. My dad is one of the *good* disbelievers. He told me it was impossible, that I'd never become world champion. He thought that champions were superhuman, and he'd simply never seen the best side of me.

I proved him wrong and I kept going. Nobody believed me at first. Nobody but me, in fact, and even I had doubts. I was scared of being wrong. Then I met Kristof and others who taught me that it's all about inventing life. It's about taking your strengths and doing something with them. It's using your tools the *right* way. If I give you three lines and ask you to make a triangle, it's impossible to make a square. I had some genetic predispositions, but John Danaher will tell you that he's seen better athletes. From my childhood skirmishes, I carried some rage that fired me up before my earliest fights, but what I acquired early on was the work ethic, discipline and good sense to listen to those who knew more than me.

MASTER: *I'm the youngest in my family and, in a sense, Georges is the little brother that I never had. And I'm the big brother he never had. Sometimes I look at him and he's the same kind, naive kid I knew ten years ago. It can be a curse in business relations, for example, but it's also what makes him distinctive and charming. He's changed in some respects. Most people are governed by self-interest, and he understands that now; he's had some painful lessons along the way. He's still got that earthy, country-boy charm. He's not nearly as naive as he once was, and he sees the darkness in the minds of men.*

Show me a hundred people and I'll show you ninety-nine with an empty, unrealistic dream. Georges didn't just have the dream, he had the plan of action to think about the circumstances to make the dream possible. Dreams on their own are utterly useless, but allied to a workable plan of action [they] garner the greatest of results, and that's exactly what Georges had from the earliest days. You saw that plan of action. Getting on a bus in the middle of a Montreal winter to ride to New York City and a godforsaken gym. Spending nights next to weed-smoking lunatics, fighting for a place to sleep. A crazy plan, but in the end, it became real. In the end, Georges St-Pierre is the only student I've ever had who taught me more than I taught him.

Ultimately, though, I'm doing what I love doing. Without that, belts don't matter.

Book 4

MAVEN

The Standing Book

WITH
Firas Zahābi, Coach

Taking a little breather between rounds. RICHARD SIBBALD

Celebrating a new UFC contract over lunch with UFC co-owner Lorenzo Fertitta (*left*). ERIC WILLIAMS

Entering the octagon in an empty Rogers Centre the night before UFC 129.
ERIC WILLIAMS

Last moments before the fight. Without my opponent, there is no me. That's why I pray for the both of us.
JOSH HEDGES/ZUFFA LLC/UFC/GETTY IMAGES

You always learn from the great Freddie Roach. ERIC WILLIAMS

Trainer Patrick Beauchamp (*right*) reminding me why I'm a beginner gymnast.
ELIDA ARRIZZA/SID LEE

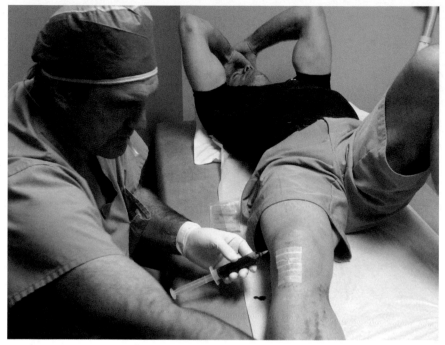

Under the expert hands of Dr. Neal ElAttrache, the man who fixed my knee.

On my road to recovery with Gavin MacMillan at Sport Science Lab.

ERIC WILLIAMS

Practice makes perfect. ERIC WILLIAMS

Canadian Prime Minister Stephen Harper offers GSP-signed gloves to his
counterpart, Japanese Prime Minister Yoshihiko Noda. JASON RANSOM

The GSP "brand" on stage at the Cannes Lions International Festival of Creativity. SORAYA URSINE/CON/LATINCONTENT EDITORIAL/GETTY IMAGES

Talking tactics with Muay Thai coach Tidiani Biga (*right*) in preparation for UFC 154. RICHARD SIBBALD

With Greg Jackson, John Danaher, Phil Nurse and Firas Zahabi. There is no championship belt without them. JOSH HEDGES/ZUFFA LLC/UFC/GETTY IMAGES

With Brazilian Jiu-Jitsu coach Bruno Fernandes (*left*) and my old training partner and manager Rodolphe Beaulieu (*right*). Rod received his black belt right after Bruno gave me my first stripe. GRACIE BARRA MONTRÉAL

"Silence is a true friend who never betrays." —Confucius

ERIC WILLIAMS

A punch starts in the feet.

My feet are the most powerful, important parts of my body, but for most of my life I ignored them. For most of my life, my feet were dead. Until I had to fix my knee.

My feet keep me balanced, centered, and they represent everything I stand for—literally and figuratively. My feet are the genesis of all my power. They're the beginning. Yet for most of my existence, for a lot of my training, for years and years of repetitions and exercises, they've been almost useless to me. In fact, when I was a little kid, I walked on my tiptoes. Over time, this caused me to walk with my feet pointing out, like a duck, and because of that I was losing power. I was losing explosiveness and balance.

Essentially, I've let my feet down. We all do, but for me it was quite important that I change that.

Never was this more evident than when I beat Matt Hughes in our title rematch. We were boxing mostly, and when he went low I caught him in the head with a left kick that dropped him, stunned. I finished with fists and elbows, but I won because of my feet.

This truth about feet and their power is so old that most human beings have forgotten it ever existed. We're too busy wearing shoes we think are comfortable—shoes we believe "support" our weight—to even think about the meaning of our feet, their purpose in our lives. But the truth is, without proper feet, there is no proper punching, or lunging, or dodging, or basic movement.

Until the invention of shoes, human beings always walked barefoot. We were, and are, primates. Our closest relatives, like it or not, are the great apes. And in the past, just like apes, we "wore" bare feet, which meant we had more sensation, more control. Our feet were better tools, like our hands are today. And we train our hands all the time. Why is that?

Although most of us are better with one hand more than the other, we know we can train ourselves to become ambidextrous. Larry Bird, the great basketball player, could dribble the ball with both hands by the time he was four years old. Tim Raines, the great Expos outfielder, was one of the best switch-hitters of all time—he could hit from both the left and right sides of the plate. Da Vinci and Michelangelo, artists of another kind, were ambidextrous too. This isn't just a coincidence or a divine gift. It's the result of years of practice and perfection, combined with the relentless development of skill. So why not practice more with our feet?

Shoes kill the sensations in our feet, which affects stability. You start compensating for your lack of balance with your knees, hips and other parts of your body. This is not good. It's bad, in fact, because it leads to various kinds of joint and structural pains that evolve with time.

Did you know that our toes and feet can keep our balance better than anything else? They keep us centered. Every single movement we make starts with our feet. Feet are the genesis of all movements, especially in mixed martial arts. It's where most of our power comes from.

Think about it and try it: if your feet are not well positioned on the ground, how can you effectively change direction? If your base is not well positioned, you have to move one of your feet first, then apply pressure to generate movement, then move the other foot, and only then can you generate any kind of power or momentum. This sounds a lot like walking, I know. In the octagon, or on the basketball or tennis court, or when you're running after a ball or trying to deke your opponent, walking isn't the solution. It takes time and it wastes energy. By being in the right position to begin with, you save time and energy, and you maximize power.

In most situations, I can't afford to lose even a fraction of a second. That's what happens when you become better at something—your margin of error is reduced. The better you get, the less room for error there is. In my sport, a fraction of a second is the difference between someone who is considered fast and someone who is considered slow. Winning and losing. Champion and has-been.

I used to lift all kinds of weight with and for my legs, but my feet weren't even an afterthought. My feet were essentially dead. I had no real sensation there. Those days are over. Ever since I started my recovery from knee surgery, I've been working on my feet. Why? Well, as the ancient Greeks believed, my soul is in my feet.

The first time a human being wore shoes was about 10,000 years ago, according to historians, and those were sandals. Considering that man (*Homo sapiens*) has been walking the earth for, oh, about 200,000 years, it's safe to say that shoes are a relatively recent invention.

What it means to me, then, is that humans before the invention of shoes were more closely connected to the earth than we are. Like in so many facets of modern life, we've become disconnected from the planet we live on.

Think about this: there are over 7,200 nerve endings in each of your feet. This means that, if your brain is the computer, it gets information from over 7,200 sources placed on each foot. The kind of critical information that determines where you stand, which direction you must move in, registers what is happening all around you and helps to get you where you want to go.

Yet every time you wear shoes or sandals, you're breaking your connection to the ground. You're losing valuable information, intelligence. Your information circuit is broken and your power potential is completely diminished. This may not be a big deal if you're sitting at the computer all day, but if you're interested in any kind of physical activity, it makes a big difference.

So training with anything other than my bare feet just doesn't make much sense to me anymore.

I became increasingly interested in feet ever since I had to rehabilitate my knee and rebuild my core strength. I started studying what Russia's Olympic coaches and athletes have been practicing and perfecting since the early 1950s, training barefoot and the like. I thought, *If I'm going to change how I use and train my feet, I want to know how other people did it before me. If I can learn from their mistakes, I'll shorten my path to important knowledge.*

There are all kinds of interesting stories related to feet. Greek gods were always portrayed barefoot. In religion—whether it's Islam, Christianity, Judaism or Buddhism—there are rituals and beliefs that say going barefoot is superior, especially for purification purposes. Art may be the best example of how feet have expressed humanity. In art, demons' feet are different from ours, they're hoofed or crooked or turned the wrong way. Angels, meanwhile, are usually in their bare feet . . .

To many cultures, the foot represents the soul. If you stop and think for a second, this makes a lot of sense—other than the obvious pun. The foot supports the entire body and keeps it standing, keeps you upright.

The foot means a lot of things, and spiritually it represents the key to all our individuality. Leaving your footprint somewhere represents something about who you are, your chosen path to advance through life, and where you have been. It connects your entire history—one step at a time—to the present. And remember: we're all moving toward a place that represents who we imagine we want to be in our future. Maybe this is why Buddhists revere what they believe are Buddha's footprints. They like to imagine where he walked so they can be inspired by his path.

The elementary truth is that feet are all about posture; they determine how you carry yourself. They play a role, whether you slouch or stand upright with your shoulders rolled back. When people look at you, they may not see your feet, your foundation, but the way you present yourself certainly has an effect on their perception. They say that body language is more than 90 percent of how people interpret others. That's another reason why feet are so important, and we see the role they play in all kinds of specialized disciplines—whether it's kung fu, karate, *savate,* Muay Thai, Brazilian Jiu-Jitsu, or even chakra meditation, reflexology, Tai Chi and just ordinary walking.

You might be thinking this is a tad eccentric—in our modern world and after years of wearing padded shoes everywhere for everything, there is something weird about the idea of doing more things in our bare feet. And don't get me wrong: I'm not planning on walking in downtown Montreal in my bare feet. But we wear padding on our feet because we don't know how to use them properly anymore. And the dirt . . .

I said earlier that humans have been around for about 200,000 years, but our predecessors, well, they've been here for over four million years. That's how long it has taken to develop the human foot. And in just a few thousand years, and with one singular object—a shoe—we've reversed the progress and changed the form and use of our feet.

And yet, there's a lot more to our feet than their history.

Some people will say, "Georges, it hurts when I run and my heels hit the ground!" That's because your heels aren't even supposed to hit the ground when you run—even if you're wearing a shoe. The whole idea of a heel strike is a mistake. It's counterproductive.

The human foot is a fabulous work of engineering. Compared to other living things, our feet are amazing just because of the way the bones and muscles are assembled and the way they've evolved over time. Shoes just constrain us and stop us from developing our feet the right way.

Even though I've neglected training my feet, I've been pretty lucky in most of my fights. In my stance, my heel almost never touches the ground, except for when I'm resting. For me, this brings my weight onto the balls of my feet, and that's where I have an advantage over most of my opponents: I'm always ready to explode or change directions.

Try jumping high. You can't do that from your heels; you have to do it from the balls of your feet. If you're well balanced on the balls of your feet, you don't have to waste time shifting your weight. You go. You save time. A fraction of a second means a lifetime. A lot of other guys stand up straight, especially the Muay Thai fighters. Recognizing this has been very important to me. It has given me an edge.

* * *

So much has changed from the early days of my career until now. When I look back at the first time I fought Matt Hughes, I see a different person—another fighter, really. First of all, I was a major, major underdog. Matt was by far the best fighter in MMA, a true legend in every sense of the word, and someone I looked up to for all kinds of reasons. He was, in my mind and pound for pound, the best fighter in the world.

I was just a kid, a kid with a title shot against his idol. I had just started training with Firas, and we had almost no resources to prepare for the title fight. Up until that point, I'd been fighting part time because I also had to make money to pay for rent and my car. I had no training partners, few coaches, and at five foot nine and 155 pounds, Firas—my sparring partner—is not a Matt Hughes replica, so my training camp was a bit of a joke.

In those days, Firas and I would work out at Tristar. It was less than half the size it is now, and my approach was not what anyone would call scientific. No one was giving us a chance to even come close to winning that fight, and to be honest with you, I wasn't sure myself how I could legitimately win.

One thing was for sure: if I beat him, it wasn't going to be easy. Before the fight, I was thinking that maybe I'd get lucky and catch him with a flying knee. Or maybe I'd take a different kind of gamble and score a big shot. Or he'd make a mistake and I'd get lucky. What that really means is that for my first fight against Matt Hughes, there was no real game plan.

A real training camp today is totally different. We have various fighters playing different roles, partners and coaches who fly in from all over the world to take part in the training camp. Back in the day, nobody wanted to touch me with a ten-foot pole. I was just a nobody, so there was no reason to be there. Matt Hughes would destroy me. In the octagon before the fight even started, I couldn't look Matt Hughes in the eye. He wasn't just intimidating, I shrank before him.

MAVEN: *To me, Georges is an ant. Everything he does can be compared to ants and how they live, what their existence is about. First of all, Georges is always going somewhere. He always has a place to go. He never stops moving, he never stops doing things that will get him closer to his goal, no matter what. And that's because he's part of a greater idea.*

Organizing my preparation is one major reason why Firas is my full-time coach. I've known him a long time. Before he was my training partner, I started training with his brother Ahmad, a Brazilian Jiu-Jitsu ace (now a doctor!), but I knew that he came from good, honest, hardworking and intelligent people. It was very rough at first with Firas. We had some very good fights against each other in training. He has an extremely high level in martial arts and he's really tough. He's good in everything—he's one of the most complete fighters I've seen, and yet he's never even fought professionally, which is interesting. He's exceptional all around, he's better than many fighters I've faced in the ring too, but he's more like Pai Mei, the character in the *Kill Bill* movies by Quentin Tarantino. He's the master who doesn't fight, but *teaches* the Shaolin fighters. That's what we call him at Tristar: Pai Mei. He has that quality where he always seems to have an answer and can find ways of surprising you and teaching you new things.

MAVEN: *Georges is definitely on a mission, and he keeps proving that he can carry more than his own weight. Like an ant, the only way to stop him would be to kill him. He has no doubt, no hesitation, no confusion, no second-guessing. Obstacles will not deter him from the goal. Not a trunk; not a twig. He'll always find a way.*

Something Firas and I often discuss is that as time progresses and mixed martial arts becomes more "intelligent," great martial artists will become smaller, less physically powerful. They'll rely on muscle much, much less. As time moves forward, our mental and tactical knowledge will grow and grow, and the next generations of fighters will rely much less on physical power and much more on the "art" in martial arts. Some styles of Brazilian Jiu-Jitsu are only seventy-five years old. This is very young for a fighting art. My job, and maybe the thing I love the most about what I do, is sharing everything I know with my peers.

* * *

Before my first UFC fight, my team and I were in a sub-basement of the Mandalay Bay Hotel in Vegas, and I was a total nobody. A nobody surrounded by other nobodies, in a cramped space. The rest of the change room was occupied by gigantic early-MMA machines who were screaming and psyching themselves up for their own fights. There were a half dozen guys at least six foot five, 250 pounds each. Rico Rodriguez, Wes Sims, Kevin Randleman, Bill Goldberg, Mark Coleman, their own teams, my two guys, and me, in the equivalent of a small kitchen. Some party.

A bunch of oversized killers, screaming and egging each other on. I was wide-eyed and freaking out. Mark Coleman was the Pride Fighting champion and I was thinking, *Wow, Coleman is in my changing room.* We thought he and his entourage would be the consummate professionals. While I warmed up in a toilet stall—doing jumping jacks in front of a toilet bowl because it was the only space left for me—they pumped up by shouting.

"YEAHHH THAT'S WHAT YOU DO FOR A LIVING, BUST PEOPLE UP! YEAH!!!"

As I was finishing my toilet-stall jumping jacks, the legendary Burt Watson kicked the locker room door in and screamed as loud as he could: *"ST-PIERRE! YOU'RE UP NEXT!"* I didn't know what was happening. This was my first rumble, and I'd never been to this planet before.

I entered the ring, put my fists up and won by unanimous decision. When I came back to the changing room, Coleman and Kevin Randleman picked me up and tossed me in the air, about six inches from the ceiling. Then they started hugging me, and then the other guys slapped me on the back and I almost went down, face-first. It felt good. Scary, but good.

My team and I decided to go out and watch Wes Sims fight, see how his guys cornered him—see how *the professionals* did it.

It was a mess. Nothing was organized or seemed ready. They even forgot to bring out his mouthpiece and had to go back while everyone waited. Then, when Wes was in the ring, his corner would just keep screaming the same three things over and over again: *"BLAST HIM, SQUEEZE HIM, KILL HIM."* And these were, at the time, the best MMA guys on the planet. Coleman was the Pride Grand Prix champion. *The King.*

And then lightning struck: Sims got beat. Rodolphe and I looked at each other and we rushed back to the locker room to get our stuff before they had the chance to get back in. I mean, before his fight, Sims's guys were punching the walls and going nuts, so I couldn't imagine what it would be like after the loss. We gathered all our stuff and got out as quickly as possible.

I saw Coleman later that night, staring at a table, his chin in the palm of his hand. He was losing it, whispering to himself, "I'm okay, I'm okay, I'll be okay," and then he'd start screaming, *"I'M SO FUCKING MAD! HE SHOULD HAVE BEAT HIM!"* He'd pound the table with his formidable fist and then he'd lower the volume again. "I'm not mad I'm not mad, he's young, he'll learn from it, it is what is, *BUT JESUS HE COULD HAVE DONE BETTER I CAN'T FUCKING BELIEVE IT,* but I'm not mad I'm not mad."

Even so, every time we return to the Mandalay Bay in Vegas, we find that dressing room and remember what that day was like. We can only laugh. We thought we were going to the big show—that it was going to be ultra-professional . . .

As it happens, I saw something else that day: Wes Sims, a six-foot-eight giant who had some pretty serious rivals, defeated mentally and tactically. I saw size, in many ways, as a detriment.

What you realize at a certain point is that physical strength has limits. It's a technological truth. Take a car jack, for instance. If you want to build a better jack, you can, and it will be stronger. But will it help you fix your car better? I don't think so. Once your car is off the ground twelve inches, the car jack's use is fully exploited. Intelligence at some point must prevail and take over from physical strength.

Humanity's true purpose is not to become stronger *physically,* it's to become more *intelligent*—from armies, who increasingly fight with specialized units rather than regiments and tanks, to garage owners, who use a lot more than jacks to fix your engine. As intelligence prevails throughout humanity, maybe there'll be fewer wars and better cars.

MAVEN: *Think about it, and remember that we all play with ants when we are kids. They're everywhere. They thrive in almost any ecosystem, they can modify almost any habitat and adjust it to their ultimate goal, they can tap into any resources they can find, and they can definitely defend themselves. All those things remind me of Georges in some way.*

Right before my first fight against Matt Hughes, after the weigh-in, Firas asked me if I was afraid of him. I lied. I said, "Fuck, no, I'm not scared." But he looked into my eyes and saw something different. He sensed it. And I paid for it later. I didn't fight the way I wanted to. The way I knew how to fight. The way I should have fought.

The next time I faced Hughes, Firas told me, right before we went into the octagon, to make sure I looked straight into his eyes, no blinking, no wavering. He knew that, from the first time around, Hughes had probably seen my fear too, and that I couldn't afford to give him that edge a second time. Because of those few seconds, everything changed for me. And they probably changed for my opponent too.

In between my Hughes fights, my fear delivered one of the great lessons of my life: that someone *without* fear can't push himself. He can't get better. He can't transform negatives into positives. He can't open his world to creativity and invention, or progress.

"He's not that good."

That was all I read. All I heard. All else was deleted. That stuff gets to you. I started doubting myself, wondering if they were right about me. It took me a long time. Until Matt Hughes, I had no confidence. It took me two fights to recover from the mental doubt. But then I really beat Hughes and I felt solid as a rock. As a mountain.

So the question is: What happens when you accept and embrace your fear? *Fear becomes your weapon.*

Some people are totally incapable of seeing fear as an opportunity to get better at something. To develop the best version of themselves. Some people wallow in their fears and try to suck their friends into the pit with them. I don't really like hanging out with these people because they suck all the good energy out of me.

Instead of seeing fear as an opportunity, they use words like *problem* or *crisis*. They're always talking about bad stuff they're "going through" and how hard it is to just get by. I don't see the use in this kind of mental discouragement. There are so many people out there who want to bring others down, that I don't need "friends" to make it worse. I want my friends to help me look at *possibility*.

This doesn't mean my friends should bullshit me about how great everything is, but the key is looking at problems as opportunities to find new solutions. This is where we learn how to *invent* life—by removing the BS, looking at the plain facts hard and directly, and then moving forward.

MAVEN: *Ants have three major qualities that connect directly to Georges and the way he goes about life. 1) They're industrious: they constantly find new ways of doing things related to their greater goal.*

What I need is a challenge, the opportunity to become a greater fighter and a greater champion. What I need is to stand in front of my faithful fans in the octagon and prove to them that they're right to support me. I want to foster pride. Respect is the title I seek.

MAVEN: *2) They're cooperative: they know that goals are most easily and efficiently achieved when they work within a team approach.*

After my loss to Matt Serra, I asked Firas to become my *head coach*. I've been undefeated since we joined forces. He's quite intelligent, he adjusts to me, he doesn't want to make me fit his mold, he doesn't have a preconceived notion of what I should become as a fighter. Simply, he wants to give me what I need to become the best I can be—*he's not looking to create a copy of himself.* This means that we work based on a system of growth that understands how learning comes from anywhere. I have different strengths and weaknesses than he does. We improve my strength and work on my weaknesses. He's a brilliant man. I learn from guys like him, not just about fighting, but about life. I love learning from people. It's very important to me.

A good fighter knows how to pick his entourage and fill it with qualified people. You need good people around you. I can't negotiate a thing. I once made an offer to buy a condominium and I offered more than was being asked. Rodolphe would have told me right away how stupid that was. Being smart is knowing what you're not good at, and finding someone who is. I have to be surrounded by people who are better than me. You need to hire to your weaknesses so you can focus on your strengths. I knew I could recover from the knee injury and re-enter the octagon because I've climbed that mountain before. Twice so far in my career, I've had to fight for and gain my world title—against Hughes and then against Serra. So I decided I would do it a third time, against Condit—just differently this time. Because I believe I can, and so do the people who are truly close to me.

MAVEN: *3) they're hardworking: like Larry Holmes said, "Hard work ain't easy, but it's fair."*

My life isn't very exciting most of the time, as I told you earlier in this book. I get up and I go to the gym to work out. Then I eat. Then I work out again, get a therapeutic massage—so I can work out again later—and then I eat more. Then I go back to sleep. That's it for most days, and I love it. In fact, I wouldn't know what to do other than follow this routine.

MAVEN: *His greatest ability is his perseverance. There's an understanding we have between us that results and success come from one place: hard work. We agree with Holmes. We think it's fair: you get back what you put in. People can cheat or rob you of almost any possession, but hard work belongs to you, and you alone. Georges knows that better than anyone I've ever known or heard of. So Georges's work ethic is his greatest gift.*

Do you want to know what I like best about myself? The truth is, I've become "great" at maybe only one thing: dedication. I've never been the fastest, or the strongest, or the biggest, or the quickest, or the most powerful. In life, we all discover at some point or other that there's someone else out there who's better at any single thing than we are.

I've found a way to turn what some call hard work into a game and an exercise in efficiency. I turned garbage collection into a race because it's good cardiovascular exercise, because it's good power training, and because it makes the day go by faster. Efficiency for me is an obsession, an addiction. It not only helps me get stronger, but makes things simpler. It helps me transcend my momentary negative inclinations. It gets me to the gym when I don't feel like going. The ancillary benefit is good habits. Food tastes better, too.

MAVEN: *When Georges and I work together, our facade is very cold. We appear to be focused only on the training and the practice. Everywhere we train, there's an audience of people watching every move, listening for every comment, every word. So you won't see us have heart-to-heart chats or catch us crying together. Our facade is tough and cold. It has to be. We keep emotions in check, we don't break down, and* *we hold each other by never showing fear. Our tender side is ours alone. We can't let fear in because it creates a floodgate of emotion. There's a time for emotion and there's a time for concentration and hard work. I know Georges will keep his facade right up to the end. But I've seen him in the locker room, I've been with him when there are no walls, and I've heard him on his knees praying. That's because, for part of his life, he'll always be alone.*

There is a side to Georges that almost nobody ever gets to see. But I've been there. I've seen him under fire. I've walked into the locker room at Tristar and he was in there, alone, after a training session. Close to the edge. I've seen him on his knees, holding his hands together and praying. As strong as Georges is, he's extremely fragile. We all are.

The key to regular growth and steady improvement is to constantly change what you're doing. Before the ACL injury, I have to admit that I'd grown tired and weary of my workout. It was tough going to the gym every day, and it was easy for my focus to be on anything except the work that needed to be done. I was in a rut and I knew it.

After my knee surgery my team and I decided to change my training approach completely. After looking around for the best postsurgical rehab and physiotherapy program, we found out about the Sport Science Lab (SSL) system. It's pretty simple, and when you go to their website, it states quite simply that they're trying to create the perfect athlete.

In my opinion, there are only a few trainers in the world who can deliver on that kind of promise. What I like best about the system is that it deviates from the popular philosophy that lifting heavy weights is the way to get strong. My interest is not in making my muscles bigger or stronger. My interest is in making my muscles *smarter* and more coordinated. The truth is that you don't need a big frame or a large physique to generate force or be skillful. It's actually the opposite. What you need is to refine your motor skills. The key for me is based on the balancing stability of the foot, its connection to the core, and in teaching my body to use the strength it already has and not allow it to dissipate.

It's pretty easy if you look at it objectively. If you can already squat five hundred pounds, you're strong, but will that always translate in the field when you're playing football, soccer or basketball? Maybe not. When you're lifting those weights, you're perfectly balanced—or *should* be. You know the variables, and now you have to physically put the weight up or bring it down. But on the field of play, there's an opponent with a plan of his own—a plan to throw you off balance.

When I was preparing for our rematch with Serra by watching tape, one thing that really stood out for me was that after he had surprised me, I lost my equilibrium—my balance was off as I rushed into counterattacks. I paid for my lack of understanding, my lack of balance.

Fluidity comes from sparring experience. It's like a dance—you fake certain tactics, movements, and you keep your opponent guessing. You never offer a static target—you always have to keep moving. It's like being hunted by a sniper—you don't just stand there, you have to move and feint. Don't make your opponent's life easy. Don't let him measure you up. In mixed martial arts, you see it all the time: a guy gets tired, slows down and soon goes static. Not long after that, he goes down, hard. *Especially* against a striker.

So the important thing is to teach your body to generate force in out-of-the-norm positions and postures. This doesn't mean you get to stop lifting weights or building mass and strength, but it means that once you reach a certain power level, there are better ways of helping you reach optimal performance than just lifting more weight. If you're an offensive lineman playing football, you're going to need not just the power and size, but all the stability and balance you can get.

In my sport, throwing a punch when you're on one foot is risky. It creates instability, and you have to push the punch harder to make it work. It's like pushing a shopping cart with a wobbly wheel—it's frustrating and inefficient. If you can throw the same punch and combine it with the ability to contract all of your muscles at the right time, you generate great power and maintain stability.

Stability is just so important—you need it to do anything. An easy example: when you go running without tied shoelaces, you trip. Generating all the speed in the world won't help you; in fact, it will just increase your risk or injury. You have to allow your body to generate the force by putting it in a stable position at all times—not just when you're running in a straight line.

There are two types of muscle groups:

- the prime movers: they do the bulk of the work, the lifting. They're the larger muscles, like quads, pectorals, and glutes.
- the stabilizers: they keep your joints running.

Just remember this: you're only as strong as your weakest link.

MAVEN: *I've seen him after a fight in his euphoric state. Each time he wins, it's like the first time, like a new event in his life. He never assumes the result will be in his favor. Georges knows that anybody can lose, anytime. It's just a matter of probability. We look at it like a math problem: there's always a chance of a different result, so let's put probabilities on our side.*

Everybody expects him to win. They expect perfection, something above and beyond what any human can do consistently. I've seen him on his knees whisper a sincere prayer. He doesn't want to let anybody down.

The key to effective visualization is to create the most detailed, clear and vivid a picture to focus on as possible. The more vivid the visualization, the more likely, and quickly, you are to begin attracting the things that help you achieve what you want to get done.

I think it works best in a quiet place, a spot where you can relax. Breathing is important, so take slow, deep breaths. The goal here is to let go of stress and just focus on what you want to see inside your mind. Then create the story you want to aim for, think of all the little details—how they look, how people sound, what's moving, colors, everything related to your senses.

It's really not easy. On top of doing all these things, you have to stay positive and ignore the negative things that can happen. You have to let go of the obstacles that can bring you down, because you have no control over them. A lot of people waste energy worrying about the things they can't control—that energy can be better used!

I read somewhere that sometimes it's easier to start at the end and play the story backward—it helps you get rid of the obstacles because the whole story starts with your goal being achieved.

MAVEN: *The key to Georges was to reach a point when there was no such thing as a glass half empty or half full. The glass is at half capacity, and that means something.*

Losing to Serra allowed me to grow in wisdom by a hundred years. It got my head out of the clouds. It got me back to doing the things I needed to do to stay successful. I'm talking about a very basic level here. I stopped going out, I trained harder, I stopped a lot of chitchat with other people. I saw what I had and what I needed. I saw the illusion that had built up around me, that I was different from other fighters.

The first time we met in the octagon, I was way too overconfident. Fine. The second time, the risk was actually on the opposite end of the spectrum: the real issue this time was confidence and believing I could actually win. Some people were telling me to watch out and "make sure he doesn't kick your ass again." That wasn't helpful advice. Sure, the intention was to make sure I didn't get hurt or didn't lose again, but the effectiveness of the advice was null and void. Luckily, they were wrong. The key for Serra Part II was simple: do not under- *or* overestimate him. The key was the Firas rule of capacity.

I find this is a really important lesson for young athletes, and it has to do with learning how to lose. Just because someone beat you badly the first time doesn't mean history will repeat itself. Any piece of history is made up from a collection of actions, of factors that play a role in the final verdict.

After a great defeat, we ask ourselves: What could I have done better? We don't ask ourselves: How could I have been stronger? We do this because the reason we lose is rarely ever *physical*.

When the reason for a loss is physical, the solution is simple: do more push-ups, run more intervals, lift more weights. But once you reach a certain level of performance, physical preparation must become secondary to mental and tactical preparation.

I've said it before, but it bears repeating: the first stage after losing a fight—and it could be anything you struggle with—is anger. But eventually, you have to accept the loss. Only then you can see things objectively. Only then you can observe your own mistakes, try solutions and improve.

There was no way I was going to approach the second fight the same way I went into the first one, but I needed to remember that so that I could focus on the important elements of winning.

One of the things I like best about Firas is that we talk about all kinds of things that have nothing to do with fighting. We chat about history, religion and especially philosophy. Firas is a true maven. The maven is a trusted expert. The maven understands, because the maven acquires a great deal of knowledge. And then the maven seeks to share it.

Here's one of the earliest examples of what you might call a philosophical chat. Before the Serra fight, we started talking about the glass being half-empty or half-full, and the difference between the two. Because the half-glass example is the perfect way to illustrate my Serra fights.

For the first fight against Serra, I saw the glass as being half-full—I was sure I had what I needed to do the job, and more. For the second fight, Firas was afraid I'd see the glass as half-empty—that I'd give Serra too much credit for what happened the first time. He was afraid I'd let my fears change my approach, that I'd let my fears guide my actions. Neither of these is a winning proposition.

On a certain day, we shifted the focus from half-full and half-empty to something totally different. We started talking about *capacity*. We simplified the statement and took the interpretation out of it. We realized that the glass is at half its capacity, neither full nor empty. And what happened is that we started to manage risk practically, by looking at the facts instead of listening to people's fears and emotions. We looked at Serra's real strengths and real weaknesses, and we were honest about them.

So we learned to manage risk by focusing on our strategy to be aggressive rather than paralysis by analysis. This was important, because the time between the two Serra fights was really,

really hard on me psychologically. After losing to Serra, a lot of people started wondering if I had a chin at all, and whether or not all of my success had been a fluke. It started in the media with certain journalists, but soon it trickled down everywhere, right into my head. I started wondering if I had a chin, if I could really take a punch, if I deserved to fight for another title. Again, I was haunted by the Serra loss for many, many months.

I didn't get to fight Serra right after losing to him. That's not how the system works. The system is based on an icy hill that takes you back down to the bottom, and you have to work your way back up. Luckily for me, I was able to hide my insecurity and lack of confidence and fight my way back to the proper mental state. The only way to ever truly get your confidence and swagger back, I've learned, is to fight for them.

In the ensuing fights, we had already decided to be different, and to use my arsenal of weapons better so that I could impose my rhythm from the start, and challenge the opponent to follow it.

We got all the facts we could on Serra, and then we took a structured, strategic approach to work. Much to everyone's surprise—given how good Serra was known to be on the ground— I took him down. And I didn't let him back up until the ref stopped the fight in round two.

In our modern world, psychologists might compare this technique to what they call cognitive therapy. Your brain is like a computer; it's connected by a bunch of networks that serve various functions. Fear likes to mess with these functions. So after a while, fear can take over the brain's networks to trigger fear reactions.

Fear likes to become one of your habits. Like being scared of dogs. Let's say you were bitten by a dog when you were a kid, so as a result it's normal to be afraid of dogs. That's what the brain tells your body every time you see a dog. Do most dogs bite people? No. But you can't expect your brain to see things that way, because the fear is telling it that dogs bite, which is based on a fact. The problem is that it's just one fact from one single occasion a long time ago. Fear doesn't study history or frequency. It cares only for itself.

Over time, you'll get better at two things: realizing it's not as bad as it is, and reducing the frequency of this kind of fear.

Don't worry, you won't ever run out of fears; you'll just get better at leveraging their power to make you stronger and better. And when you tell a negative, fearmongering friend to stop it, tell him it's part of your fear training program. Who knows, maybe you'll help him or her get better too. Just remember that you may wish to learn to deal with your own fear before you can share your friends'.

MAVEN: *In his position, Georges is on the receiving end of all kinds of negative energy. There are insults, threats and taunting, but we just work to turn those into motivational fuel. What Georges is able to do, because he's patient and thoughtful and strategic, is hold on to those insults and taunts so he can use them later. You won't see him lose his temper at a press conference or anywhere else; he'll use other people's negative energy to fuel his training and workouts. Those workouts are the ones that determine who's going to win on fight night, because a fight is much longer than five rounds. A fight takes place over many weeks and months.*

A lot of people ask me: How many hours does it take to build a GSP? But it's not like baking a pie. You can't just gather the basic ingredients and mold them into a world champion. It takes a supreme kind of individual, one who is willingly dedicating his entire life to a greater goal. It takes someone willing to put himself through torturous amount of

pain. It's more like going to space—you have to be ready for
so many different eventualities and various kinds of strains
and pressures. Not anybody can be an astronaut—there are
multitudes of tests before sending someone into space. Well,
not anybody can become a mixed martial artist—and cer-
tainly not anybody can become a world champion. Almost
anybody can be greatly successful. However, most people are
not willing to go through the process and [they] simply want
the result. It's having to go through the process that stops peo-
ple, not their limited potential.

My mistakes torment me. I torture myself going over and
over and over again about what I did wrong so that I never do it
wrong ever again, and the result of my efforts to date has been
a real reversal of fortune. I may have lost that first battle against
Hughes, but I was fortunate enough to fight and beat him two
more times afterward, so you could say I won the war.

It's all part of my process, what Firas calls my "premise."

There is an overarching premise for the "machine" my team
and I are trying to build. We've been working on it for years
now, and we spend a lot time discussing the big idea behind all
my training and the things we need to do to bring us closer to
the ultimate level. What I mean by "the ultimate level" is a system, like a machine, that performs to the best of its capacities
in any situation. The purpose, of course, is to triumph inside
the octagon.

Before getting to the system itself, we need to understand
that there are many ways to fight inside the octagon. Regardless
of the "way"—the preferred method for any individual—there
is an even simpler truth: there are really only two kinds of
fighters: the specialist and the generalist.

The best example of the specialist may be Jon Jones. Jon has the longest reach of any fighter in MMA history. That makes him a striker—a freak of nature in many ways, one who can outstrike anybody (in addition to having great wrestling skills). Anyone who stands against Jon and tries to exchange punches is in very deep trouble. Another good example of a specialist is Matt Hughes, who is lethal when he gets you on the ground to grapple or wrestle. That's why I generally tried to fight Matt Hughes standing up—on the ground, the advantage would always be his, as it was in our first fight.

A specialist can be as dangerous as an all-around guy, and more so on some occasions because specialists are gifted. It's in the name—they're *special*. So a specialist is someone with an extreme gift—speed, power, reach, impulse, explosiveness—who turns it into a unique weapon.

And then there is the generalist, which is what my whole system is based on. Firas often says, "The king of all styles is the antagonist." By antagonist, he means generalist, someone who causes trouble from any of the fighting stances. The reason is simple: when you're a generalist, you try to provoke your opponent so he gets out of his comfort zone, away from his specialty. I always aim to antagonize my opponent and dictate the rhythm of the fight, and where it will take place inside the octagon.

So for a generalist, if you fight a wrestler, you have to box him. If you face a boxer, you have to wrestle him. This is the main premise to my system: whatever my opponent does best, I will try to take him to the other realm. I will try to take him out of his comfort zone and into mine, which can be any of the three ways of fighting. That's what I did against Hughes in the two follow-up fights. I kept him away from his strength.

Yet it takes more than just being a good all-around generalist to defeat a specialist. After all, he's trying to get you into his space so that he can focus on his specialty, and at this stage in his career, he's probably pretty good at it. Luckily, although the wrestlers are the kings of mixed martial arts, there is one advantage for the generalist: all fights start standing up. The wrestler needs to get close enough to you to bring you down to his strength, and that's not always easy.

We practice a lot of kickboxing to deal with ground specialists, because it's the only way I know to dictate to a wrestler where the fight will be fought.

The big lesson here is this one: fight his weaknesses and avoid his strengths.

> **MAVEN:** *If they tried Georges's training regimen, I think a lot of people would break down psychologically. It's not for everybody. Not everybody can withstand it. There's a reason that there's only one Rome . . . if it was easy, they'd have built more of them!*

I have to make my training harder and more challenging than my next fight. The reason, quite simply, is to create extreme conditions to ensure that I'm ready for anything. So training with winners, with guys who are better than me at specific elements of martial arts, will make me a better all-around fighter. It will make me more rounded. I figured out a long time ago that I would never become the best at a single thing. I couldn't be the fastest guy, or the strongest, or the most agile. But I discovered and understood how I could probably become the best *all-around* fighter and athlete, so I focused on that. I focused on my strengths.

So I spend most of my time training with people who are better than me. Especially when I'm preparing for a fight. If my next opponent is an excellent wrestler, for example, I'll spend a great deal of time practicing with wrestling experts who are better at it than I am. I'll go to my Montreal wrestling coach Victor's gym to face the best there is. Or if I'm up against a left-handed fighter who's got a great left hook, I'll spend many hours in the ring facing left-handers who pack a lot of power in their punch.

One of the ways to get better is to focus on other people's strengths and learn from them, which is why I like to train with specialists. Specifically, training with winners means that I always, *always* have to focus 100 percent, lest, quite frankly, someone—probably me—gets hurt. So, even in training, I can't afford to dog it or take it easy, because not only will I be on my back all the time, I just might wind up with a torn ACL.

Just the fact that I have to be at 100-percent focus triggers other training necessities. The first one is stress. If I have to go all out in training, it means constant stress and pressure to perform, to focus and to deliver. Even though I try to train with people better than myself at various aspects of the fight game, the last thing I want—when I'm in the gym, on the mat, in the ring or inside the octagon—is to be seen losing all the time. But learning how to handle that kind of stress—the stress to earn and keep people's respect—makes me ready to handle other kinds of stress. We try to create situations that are out of the ordinary so that, after time and repetition, they become part of my routine. And then I keep elevating the intensity and build higher.

MAVEN: *Georges's trainability is amazing. It is where he becomes unique, incomparable to any other fighter or athlete. It's not about any one kind of mentality at this stage. The key is just being completely open-minded and immersed in learning, no matter the learning. With Georges, it's never about liking or not liking a certain kind of training—it can't* *be. And that's the difference maker. Most people do what they like to do, and they avoid doing what they need to do. Mastering all forms of the fighting sciences is exceptionally difficult. Sometimes, it's really unpleasant. It requires dedication and confidence, and a person who can absorb all the extra information. That's Georges. He takes it all in, processes it and keeps the valuable information so he can use it anytime. The reality is that you don't get to take that many breaks when you're part of a great goal, and people need breaks from stuff, from life. Georges, though, he does it when he has to do it, not just when he feels like doing it.*

I have a friend who has a great idea about training. He says, "You don't get better on the days when you feel like going. You get better on the days when you don't want to go, but you go anyway." This makes a lot of sense. It's easy to go and train when you feel like it. Your body and your mind are in sync and they deliver because it feels so natural. But when your body is telling you it doesn't want to go because it's in pain or it's tired, or when your mind is trying to convince you to go out drinking with friends or stay home and watch TV, this means trouble. But—and it's a big but—if you can overcome the negative energy coming from your tired body or unmotivated mind, you will grow and become better. It won't be the best workout you have, you won't accomplish as much as what you usually do when you actually feel good, but that doesn't matter. Growth is a long-term game, and the crappy days are more important.

The best part is at the end of your workout on the crappy day. You feel better about yourself, happier and proud. Food tastes better and you feel like you earned the reward of a delicious protein shake or a healthy, reconstructive meal. The best part is mental too, because now you know that you have the power and the resolve to vanquish negative thoughts and challenge yourself to do better. Knowing I'm in control means my foundation is strong, and that right there is an unstoppable force of energy.

The next logical step of the process is confidence. When you understand how to piece the key elements of your training together, you become all-powerful in your mind. This kind of belief is inestimable and immeasurable. People who believe in themselves can accomplish almost anything. And one thing is for sure, they can become even more powerful—but it all begins with the *attitude*.

MAVEN: *I've seen Georges in his most honest hour. As strong as he is, as powerful and skillful and dominant as he has been, he trains so much because there's a fear of losing. We train to eliminate all those vulnerabilities. The reality is that eliminating one vulnerability only reveals a new one. It may not be as bold or threatening as the previous one, but it's there. Once we discover it, we must work to eliminate it. This is perfectly normal behavior, if you ask me, but it's rare in people. Some guys think they're so good, they don't train as much as they should. Life wins against those guys. Georges is the opposite. It's a painful experience, it's constant torment, it's the cycle of fear and how it walks alongside even the most fearsome individual. But it's also what keeps Georges moving forward.*

A shift enters my world in the weeks and days before a fight, and I always feel a gradual pull toward the octagon. I sense a force, an energy source that moves and changes me. I believe this force turns me into the warrior I need to be to perform, to do my job, to fight in the octagon and to emerge the victor.

I also know, better than most, that what I do for a living is different. I know it's odd and distant to many people in the world. And I understand that most people have scarcely any idea of what exactly it is I'm doing in that ring, in tights and cut-off gloves, fighting for my livelihood. I know these things because I feel them. I'm aware of them in my sphere, my existence. I've been confronted by them ever since I wanted to fight, when my own parents questioned what I wished to do with my life.

It's why, in the days before a fight, I retreat into a space that is all my own. I fall back into a position, a preparation, that allows my mind and my soul to process what is about to happen. As the day of reckoning approaches, the truth is that I avoid most of my friends and family. I shun them. I avoid their calls. I ignore their messages. I can hardly stand to have them near me. I can't have them and their normal lives impacting what is about to happen. I need to be near other warriors. I need their company, their presence, their aura, their chatter. Sometimes we talk, and other times we sit in total silence. But always, we are in the company of men who have entered the ring the same way I am about to: alone, vulnerable, fierce and determined.

I need to be in contact with fighters who understand the feeling of facing another man in a physical confrontation. This kind of unique, epic battle against other martial artists demands time. A special kind of worship. So that my mind will allow me to fight, to strike and to vanquish. So that I can calibrate to what needs to be *my* normal. So I can enter the octagon.

A lot of the prefight preparation is serious and, as above, almost spiritual. Visualization allows me to come in and out of focus, to turn my brain on and off and maintain a balance. To be prepared without overthinking.

The rest of it is either boring—or funny. You can't take yourself *too* seriously.

As for the boring part, you're trying to make weight, you're sitting around with your coaches and other fighters, and you spend a lot of time in your hotel room, reading or watching movies. I get the funny part from all sorts of movies, our two favorites being select scenes from *Full Metal Jacket* and *Kill Bill 2*. Firas and I like the opening scene from *Full Metal Jacket,* when the drill sergeant greets the new recruits. It's just crazy that there really are people like that in the world. Granted, the *rest* of the movie isn't much of a comedy . . .

Our favorite movie scene to watch before a fight is "Chapter 8: The Cruel Tutelage of Pai Mei," from Quentin Tarantino's *Kill Bill 2*. Essentially, it's a surreal part of the story that addresses three key topics in martial arts, *à la* Tarantino: science, philosophy and, of course, fighting.

A young woman whose character is named The Bride (played by Uma Thurman) meets Pai Mei, a grand master of kung fu. She tells him that she's not completely untrained, that she's an expert in the art of the samurai sword. The grand master smirks; she feels ridiculous. He scrutinizes her; she is reduced. He challenges her to a duel, promising to call her Master—if she defeats him. Obviously, she loses, and realizes that she's like a worm fighting an eagle.

It's funny as hell, but if you go back and watch the scene, you'll see it ties to the Socratic method: give me a premise that you believe in, and I will cross-examine you. You'll say you know something, and I'll cross-examine your conclusion. In the end, if there's any contradiction, your premise becomes invalid. It means that if my line of thinking is wrong, my conclusion can't be true.

Over the years, Firas and I have discussed this many times. Our own understanding is that Socrates never claimed knowledge; he was *pursuing* it. He could never really be sure of anything except awareness of his own ignorance. It's about how much higher an individual needs to go. No matter how good you are, you're always relatively weak. In the film, The Bride eventually realizes that she knows nothing. Hence, the more I know, the less I know.

I remember I once told Firas that I felt good and that I was in good shape. I was convinced I couldn't get much more fit because I felt so strong. But I was mistaken. Instead of telling me that he disagreed and that I could be fitter, Firas did something different: he took me to see gymnasts and work out with them. I quickly discovered that my level of fitness was, in many ways, totally useless. I was strong, yet I couldn't complete or properly execute any of the tests the gymnasts were performing with great ease and grace. I understood my own feeble self by being put to the test, by feeling my own clumsiness and lack of skill. The situation forced me to adopt a new mindset, thanks to how my own Pai Mei (Firas) transformed me from an eagle into a worm.

The conclusion is that one thing never changes: my mindset must be open to improvements at all times, from all sources. This kind of cruelty, the worm and the eagle, is actually kindness. It represents short-term pain for long-term benefit.

And so, in the week preceding a fight, every single day, Firas and I will sit in our hotel room and watch this specific scene from the movie.

* * *

One element of my progression as an athlete has been to understand how our bodies work. After all, arms, legs and spines are generally built the same way (for the most part). The things that makes us different are height, length and width. This is why the punching triangle I talked about earlier in the book is so important: everything is a game of angles. Working with Gavin MacMillan at SSL has helped me learn so much about the body.

The interesting thing is that some of the things I learned are very, very modern, while others have been known for centuries. Leonardo da Vinci, for example, was the first to show that human bodies are geometrically balanced. His drawing of the Vitruvian Man proves it. Da Vinci is also the person who coined this familiar phrase: "You are what you eat." We still talk about that today because it's so true. I believe that an athlete has to eat good, nutritious food to keep the motor going. In many ways, obese people are actually starving: they eat all kinds of junk with so little nutritious value that most of it gets turned into fat. The rest of the body—muscles, for example—remain starved of nutrients.

And so nutrition, to me, is not necessarily about *what* you eat. It's about the *decisions* you make when you have to eat, which translates to discipline and control. Don't get me wrong: I still love and eat dessert. There's this little Portuguese chicken place in St-Michel, in the North End of Montreal, and whenever I go, I finish my meal with a *pastel de nata*—a Portuguese custard tart that is delicious, especially when it's served warm with a hint of cinnamon. But before I get to dessert, I make sure to eat a great breast of chicken and salad (and sometimes a handful of fries). With the amount of exercise I do in a day, my body can actually afford to eat what it wants, as long as it gets the right nutrients and fuel to keep it going at peak performance.

The real test is this one: When you're alone in a room, when you're in a private place and nobody else can see you, what do you choose to do? Eat well, or eat poorly? Exercise, or watch television? Practice something, or do nothing? The best version of the truth appears to you and you alone, when nobody else can see. This is the test of discipline, and it's what makes the difference in your life. It's what regulates your own system and guides it. The individual alone comprehends it.

One of the new learnings is related to the myelin sheath, which my buddy Rodolphe is obsessed with. Basically, it's all about muscle memory. As we've discussed previously, the myelin sheath is connected to the nervous system and it works like this: the more you perform a specific gesture, the better you become at memorizing and "firing up" the perfect movement without hesitation. It's the self-invention of the human instinct.

By combining Rodolphe's muscle memory approach with Gavin's all-around approach to rehabilitation, I'm actually reconnecting my own system to perform better. The result should be a more efficient, better-rounded GSP.

What I like about this new approach is more than the physical benefits. Now, when I work out or rehab my knee, I feel invigorated. My brain feels stimulated and I'm excited that my physical training is having a positive effect on my mental outlook. I feel that by focusing on smaller parts of my body—like my feet—I'm actually working and improving my entire body.

Now I'm less worried about plateauing. Plateauing is when your body lacks motivation to push itself to new limits. When you plateau, you feel like you can't push anymore or make any more progress. You feel like your world is flat. So part of the joy of my rehab has been to discover new ways of training to stimulate new parts of my body.

The better I become at training, the more I realize how everything mental and physical is connected.

MAVEN: *One of the guys who manages his accounts told me another Georges story. He told me that Georges, because he spends to much time on the road, could easily establish his residency in another country where the tax rates are much lower than Quebec's. That it was recommended to Georges that he should do this so he could save money—just like Formula One drivers or other big international athletes do. And he refused, flat out and immediately without even thinking about it (or the money) for a second. Georges said: "I live here most of the time and I want to keep living here. I benefit from the services like everybody else, so I'm going to pay my share like everybody else."*

It's not about the titles for him. It's not about the money, either. It's about the experience and sharing the experience. Now that I think of it, and knowing what I know about Georges, I think he was already thinking about the next fight.

What's the point of all this? To say that losing the UFC title doesn't matter. That's not the ultimate goal. When the media were asking me about it when I announced the knee surgery, I told them the only thing that belts are good for is to hold up your pants.

MAVEN: *That's the heart of GSP, and people should know. It says a lot about him and his life priorities.*

Overtraining worked for me for a long time, but somewhere along the road it became detrimental and destructive. I got to the point many times when I couldn't stop myself from working out more.

When I tore my ACL, I was so intent on pushing myself that I couldn't stop anymore. I'd get up and go to work out. Then I'd eat and go to gymnastics. Then I'd get a massage and go to Tristar to train with Firas in the ring, then on the mat, and then in the octagon. I treated my body like a machine, but I forgot that even machine engines need a rest, need some fuel, and need to *relax*. I was working harder to try and rid myself of negative energy that was the result of . . . overwork. I was unhappy and mired in a negative cycle of useless repetition.

Again, like so many things I've learned in my life and have tried to share in this book, the key is finding balance. The thing about balance, though, is that it's never stagnant. It's not something you discover one day and then it stays there for the rest of your life and you live a perfect existence. It's the opposite. Finding balance is just a sign that you know how to invent your own life, but it's a lesson that keeps evolving. Especially for people like me, who are goal-oriented and curious about change and evolution.

And so, what balance also taught me are the following two incredibly important lessons: 1) resting is growing and 2) waiting is training.

What does "resting is growing" really mean? It means that you have to give your body time to recover from tough workouts, especially if you're training every day. It sounds really weird to people who work out so much, but that's because they're addicted to the workout. They can't stop. Trust me, I've been there. It's because the body and the brain are sometimes fighting battles. The body wants to rest and grow, while the brain thinks the body needs more work.

Since my knee surgery, I've started working out less and resting more. Just as a test. And oddly enough, my muscle weight is growing faster than ever before. I remember after the surgery, standing in front of the mirror and looking at my legs and how little my thighs seemed to me. They looked like they'd lost a few inches. So had my chest and arms. When I was able to return to the gym, I had a regimen to follow, and I couldn't push myself too much. I wasn't allowed, and it would have been stupid to do so. It was hard to hold myself back, to stop from going to train, or run, or fight. But I did, and one day, standing in front of the mirror, I noticed that my "things" were back, and they were my shoulders and back and chest and arms. But I'd been working out less than before.

It makes me feel so dumb for all the years I did things wrong. Now I know: resting is growing.

That's why "waiting is training" is the next part of my approach. "Waiting is training" means that I can spend more time preparing mentally for my next session or fight, and less time physically exhausting myself. By waiting, I'm sending a message that strategy is more important than pure physical power, that tactics surpass repetition, and that the brain is the most powerful muscle in the body.

* * *

There are times when hitting the bags is important, but those decrease in importance as my expertise grows. Bruce Lee talked about this a lot. Hitting the bags or the dummies is good to create muscle memory while I'm trying to perfect a movement—a punch or a kick. But it means nothing else. Once I learn a movement or a style of kick well, I need to perform it against a willing opponent.

Sometimes, it's a fighter who's better than I am—which is creating the ultimate challenge for practice. And other times, it's a fighter who's not as good as me—which is creating a winning situation that gets my body accustomed to performing against a moving target.

As I mentioned earlier, it all comes down to confidence: your body can do great things only if it believes it can accomplish them. The only way I've ever made that happen is by preparing my mind for the worst conditions possible in training, and then surpassing them. This is why I always say that fights aren't won in the octagon, they're won in the months leading up to them, in a near-empty gym, in the lost hours of a day, whether I feel like it or not.

That's training with betters and what it brings me. But I don't always train with betters, with winners. I train with lesser fighters too, with losers. I don't mean losers in the pejorative sense, but I mean that I train with people I know I'll defeat every single time I go out there. I train with people who will lose to me every single time, guaranteed.

A big part of my training is to create conditions that make survival almost impossible, but I also want to ensure to build balance by creating conditions that make my success entirely possible. I want to make sure that my body and my brain get used to doing things right and feel every movement to its fullest.

Think about it for a second, as if you're a baseball player. When a baseball player takes batting practice, he's not up there to strike out. The person throwing balls at home plate isn't trying to fool the hitter: he's trying to make the hitter feel powerful. He's trying to get the hitter to understand how to hit the ball out of the park, or safely for a base hit, with his eyes and, physically, with his whole body. The same is true for all sports—shooting open three-pointers, throwing the ball to wide-open receivers, et cetera.

Good training and preparation aren't about creating losing conditions, they're also about creating winning conditions. So at specific times during my fight preparation, my team goes out to the Gracie Barra dojo in Montreal with Bruno Fernandes, and I get to fight with a few blue belts.

First of all, this is very good for me because it allows me to practice my attacks. I have someone in front of me whom I know

I can take down quickly. So I do, and I get used to the feeling of being the aggressor. My body and mind interact and understand how to execute the movement freely, comfortably and, hopefully, to perfection.

What this means, contextually, is that I get to focus on success. I get "easy" wins in practice, and that makes me feel good. It sounds clichéed, but I'm now truly understanding that training is like life in that it can't always be hard, because then it stops being fun. With success comes timing and technique. I can repeat certain moves over and over again until they're perfect, against a willing opponent who knows just enough to make it challenging without being *too* hard. Succinctly put: training with lesser fighters lets me work on my timing.

And very basically, if an athlete constantly puts himself in losing situations, he or she can develop paranoia. An athlete has to win in practice too. He has to triumph and feel the flow of a perfectly executed movement so that his mind grows accustomed to victory.

But it's good for the lesser, too. I mean, Rodolphe and I can't just pick any blue belts in the class and put them through this training, but the ones we do pick learn from it too. They never get hurt—that's the most important thing—because my technique is pretty good now. They get to experience firsthand what it feels like to be in against a tough opponent. Maybe the most important thing for them is that they get to understand what an opponent goes through in tough situations.

The only way to truly know what it feels like to get taken to the ground and be put in an armlock is to be the victim, not the aggressor. This is an elementary rule in martial arts, and everybody who learns goes through it. You'll never understand what a punch in the head feels like if you're the one doing the punching. And while it'd be fun never to be in that position, winning fighters all know that success comes from the ability to absorb punishment.

It's not bad for my blue belts either. It puts them in new situations they can learn from It's a win-win situation for everybody involved. It's good for their confidence, and it's good for mine too. I could never win real fights if all I ever did in practice is put myself in losing situations. I'd become a paranoid being who sees disaster in every event and situation.

Whatever their skill level, though, I'm always looking for a willing opponent who's trying to beat me.

MAVEN: *After each one of Georges's title victories, he gives his belt away. He gives it to someone close to him, someone he feels helped him reach his goal. This is pure amazement to me.*

After his big fight in Toronto, in front of the biggest live audience ever to watch a UFC championship, after he had beaten the only opponent the public felt could beat him, Georges gave me his belt. We were in the octagon right after the fight, celebrating. They put the belt around his waist and he turned around and he whispered in my ear, "This one's for you." That was the biggest venue in UFC history, his crowning moment in history, and he wasn't thinking about himself. He hadn't been wearing the belt for more than five seconds—no more than five!—and he gave it away. This belt represents everything he's worked for, and then he turns around and gives it away. I can't tell you how touched I was. What an incredible thing to do. I can't say that I truly understand the gesture. I was perplexed that that's what was on his mind after his fight.

Knowing yourself lets you differentiate between luck and movement. It places them at opposite ends of the spectrum. Luck is not within anybody's control or prediction. It occurs, and it's great when it does, but you can't base your entire life on it. Movement, on the other hand, puts success within reach. The more you know about yourself, the better your movement through all facets of life.

This applies to everybody—doctors, cooks, farmers, whomever. The rule, when applied to me, is ordered by priority: 1) to stick to the things I know and do them well, and constantly improve; 2) to grow, slowly and surely, my knowledge base, to become the greatest martial artist I can ever be; 3) to get the maximum out of myself; 4) to develop my abilities into skills, because there's a great difference between the two. Ability is related potential, but skill represents the concept of doing, of movement. But I digress.

I was sitting backstage at the Cannes Creativity Festival in June 2012, before we were due to give a presentation to people in the communications and creative world who wanted to hear about the GSP "brand," the communications strategy that has allowed me to have so many followers on social media, and how I approach all of my sponsorship partnerships and my foundation against bullying. I told my team I felt like the luckiest person in the world. I get to do what I want in my life, and I can follow the path of my own choosing. Which results in something even greater than its component parts: happiness.

It's true about the belts. I gave the first one to my mom, one to Kristof, and then one to Firas. Why keep a belt? It doesn't bring me anything extra just by sitting there at home. For me, a belt is something you show off, and I'm not a showy kind of person. I keep the one I have in the closet. For Firas, Kristof— who have their own gyms and also train there—those belts have a meaning. Those belts play a role. I think it's fair recognition for all the work they've done on my team. My mother keeps hers on display. The *title* is what is meaningful to me; that's the true reward.

If you really want to know, that unicorn—the one my godmother, Madeleine Pagé, gave me before she died, when I was just a little boy—is one of the few material things that actually matter to me. It's irreplaceable. I've taken good care of it and it's still really pretty. She wrote me a letter and gave me a nice drawing before she died. I reread her words, and they make even more sense as I grow older, and wiser.

The world and its secrets *are* frightening, and there's no shame in admitting that kind of fear. It's the only way there is to face it, in any single moment. It's why I don't mind being scared: happiness.

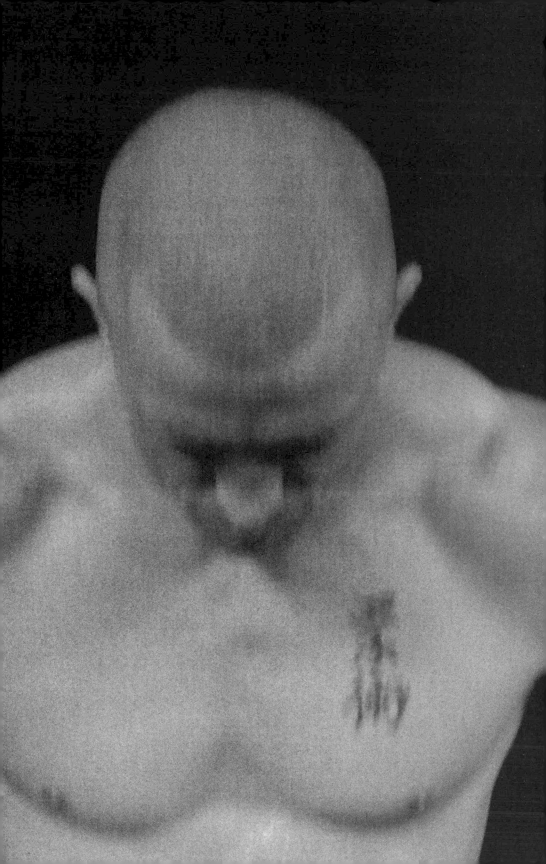

BOOK 5

....

CONSCIENCE

WITH

RODOLPHE BEAULIEU, MANAGER/FRIEND

It is bad when one thing becomes two.
One should not look for anything else in the Way
of the Samurai. It is the same for anything that is
called a Way. If one understands things in this manner,
he should be able to hear about all ways and be more
and more in accord with his own.

—Yamamoto Tsunetomo

I like being around people.

don't like solitude. I *need* to be around other humans. I crave human contact and interaction and laughter and escape.

Yet I know that this journey is unforgiving to my friends and relationships. My life, generally speaking, is organized around two events a year: a pair of fights. I can divide my existence into chunks of six months. I train, I announce my next fight and I prepare for it—that's about four months interspersed with a week on a beach somewhere. Then I enter my training camp, and the next two months are emotionally excruciating.

The closer a fighter gets to his next fight, the more he or she feels alone. None of us can help it.

CONSCIENCE: *No other person can have any understanding, any frame of reference, any clear idea of what exactly Georges is living in the weeks before the fight. Not even Firas, who possesses a mere a fraction of appreciation for it despite his brilliance and wisdom. Because he's never been in the octagon as a fighter. He's never been the world champion. He's never stepped to the threshold before millions of people, with thousands upon thousands in the arena chanting his name, knowing that one false move, a single, stupid, minor mistake, can cause the empire to crumble into rubble. That this could be the penultimate moment before the end. That everything*

rides on fractions of seconds and flashes of brilliance—or
failure. With all his knowledge, accumulated over years and
years of practice and study, there are limitations even for
Firas, and he is Georges's head coach and closest collaborator.
Only a few select people in the world understand the feeling
of stepping into the octagon, and that's because they've been
crowned, at one point or another, as UFC world champion.
It's a unique kind of trip, as if entering the octagon was ven-
turing into another dimension. Another world.

When I enter a training camp, I can't help but start to feel increasingly like I'm the only person on the face of the earth. It truly, *truly* sucks. I get home at night and there I am, alone. I take a look around me, and the silence hits. It strikes full force. It imbues my soul with this distant, ugly melancholy that carries me away from the world I know. From my friends who are out having fun, laughing, relaxing. It is, to me, the truest representation of the word *solitude*. I'd much rather be out socializing, but I can't be. I can't go out and do, well, anything.

And then, as fight night nears, it doesn't matter where I am or whom I'm with. The world around me somehow keeps its distance. It doesn't matter if I'm surrounded by people or not; loneliness forms an aura around my being, shutting me off from normalcy. Alone, in my solitude, with my own thoughts. It's unbearable.

Misunderstood and alone in the world, I try to call friends, people who can help fill my mind with other thoughts, but it's just a temporary distraction. And I don't like chatting on the phone—fidgety impatience. Any text or telephone chat is a limited reprieve because the solitude is always there, waiting for me.

In the day, though, I'm always busy. I don't fully enjoy most of the photo shoots and marketing events. There are more and more of them, admittedly, but it was even worse a few years ago, when there were fewer of them. Let me explain. Before Rodolphe joined my team, it was something I *had* to do, following the orders of people I didn't like being around. At least Rodolphe's one of my best friends, which makes it fun. I get to tease him too, because these are moments when he's more stressed than I am.

The reason I find it difficult is how it greatly affects my personal life. I like freedom. I'm the kind of guy who often does exactly the opposite of what he's been told. I've always been like that. I've always had a rebellious side, a teasing, malicious side. When cameras are present, I have to be "on" all the time. I have to be in the GSP character whenever the cameras are there. I don't change the person I am, but I present him in a different light. The result is that I censor myself. I don't share every thought that passes through my head. I don't speak *exactly* the way I normally would, and I have to be conscious of it. I can't say everything that's on my mind. I'm still me, but somehow I'm more guarded.

The closer it gets to fight night, the worse my solitude is. A living hell, a torment only Dante could have imagined. The week of the fight is insufferable. I feel covered in the wrong layer of skin. I can't wait for the fight to end. It becomes weeks of this kind of emotion, mounting, growing inside me. An emotional tumor. Before the Condit fight, Kristof came to Montreal from his place in Monaco and spent over a month living and training with me, and it just about saved my sanity.

CONSCIENCE: *The dual pressure of the fighting world is cruel, and worse than any sport. It obliges a fighter to perfectly combine his physical and mental focus, more than any other individual or team sport. In baseball, the greatest hitters of all time have a failing grade, and they play 162 games in* *a regular season. In tennis, with four majors and countless tournaments all over the world, each athlete can start over on an almost weekly basis. The same goes for golf. In football, a team can win a game even if its offense can't score, and players get to wear those funky helmets. In mixed martial arts, an established, successful fighter has two moments in a calendar year. Two moments he can't back away from. An up-and-comer fights more, for a few thousand dollars at a time, hoping to climb the ranks. Each of us follows the same path, but not many will reach the summit. This is not the fighter's tragedy, it is the fighter's reality.*

If there's a camera, I'm *on*. I know I have to somehow monitor what I say and I can't act like a clown. (But I *like* acting like a clown!) Despite knowing I have to be aware at all times of what I'm saying or doing, I've always tried to find a way to stay authentic.

I know that some people think I'm doing this for the money, but they're plain wrong. The marketing and sponsorships have a strategic purpose in my life, but finance isn't it. I have enough money in the bank to live the rest of my life. The two most luxurious items I own were given to me. And I *know* what it's like to exist based on the next $5 bill that comes into my pocket, and it's not that bad. I *know* I'll always have my parents' basement in St-Isidore to go home to, whatever happens.

CONSCIENCE: *A losing fighter can be bruised, cut into, bleed and break. A winning fighter can come out swollen and bruised and broken as well. And the next day, people look at those fighters and judge them on how they look, not just how they performed. Hence the expression, "You should see the other guy." This isn't meant to reduce the ardor of other sports—*

quite the contrary—but how quickly people forget the last eight title defenses, the number of rounds won consecutively, the statistical domination across all fighting stances. With every single loss comes great risk, because sponsors prefer champions and titles, and fickle is the nature of business. It makes for a lot of pressure, and luckily for us, Georges's sponsors have been there for the man and not just the belts.

The counterargument is that I really do care for all of my sponsors. Without them, there is no *me* in the current form. They give me the tools and the means to prepare my career and plot my future. A lot of people have asked me why I ever started all the branding work and marketing planning, and the answer is really simple: I needed help to know when to say yes and when to say no. Some companies have made me extremely lucrative partnership offers—and I mean *extremely*—but they didn't feel right. Each and every sponsor we work with is screened from top to bottom: What do they stand for? Do they just want my face, or are they looking at working together to build something? Where are they going in the future? These things actually matter to me.

When an opportunity with a sponsor comes in, we have a team meeting. My team takes me through all of their analysis, presents me with my options, and I make the final decision. I will say this for certain: if I don't like the brand or what it's doing, it's a simple, thankful no. If I see potential and there is a win-win-win situation—for them, for my fans and for me—then we go for it. It's that simple.

If I or anyone else wants to become the best at something in this millennium, none of us will get there alone. And I've always hated doing things alone.

CONSCIENCE: *My own life changes the moment Georges climbs those stairs into the ring. When I see the gate close and the lock click into place, there is nothing left for me to do. I have no more impact, no purpose. The best thing I can do (the only thing I can do) is to have a plan and be prepared for any of the two outcomes. When the gate closes, there is nothing left but to sit there, to watch and pray, to hope and cheer, when I'm capable of it. I become a fan, a follower who analyzes each moment of the fight because I can't let go of the martial artist or the fan in me. As a training partner who has seen all of Georges's fights, I can usually predict the outcome during the first minutes of the opening round—which makes those moments excruciating. There is always the possibility of an errant kick, like Condit's third-round knockdown, but nobody can predict freak occurrence. Even though I'm sitting next to the ring, I usually watch one of the big screens to ensure I have an unobstructed view. I look for Georges's movement, for the distance he maintains from his opponent, from the snap and whip in his strikes, and then I know. In the pit of my gut, I understand what the outcome should be. I can just feel it.*

When the gate closes, Georges must be left alone, to his own devices, and his opponent's. Helplessness is what I feel.

Before a fight, I'm a complete mental case, a walking stress ball. Rodolphe is my friend, and I don't know how he does this job. I'd never be able to do it. I realize now that he's protecting me so I can focus entirely on my work. He's my shield, and I don't even have to carry him around. He walks next to me, always.

And then, suddenly, the fight happens, and it's over, and a special kind of deliverance arrives in my life. I want to dance, to laugh. Life is an all-out party, and it can last for days on end. And it feels like the greatest time of all time because of the ordeal that just ended. Which means, when I pause to consider it, that one is dependent on the other.

Suffering allows you to truly appreciate release, which means there's an odd relationship with balance. When great depths of unrelenting sorrow are punctuated by great peaks of joy and liberation, the result is delicious. It's about appreciating the little things that make my life so great—a glass of water, eggs and bacon, a slice of chocolate cake. Getting tipsy. To truly understand the greatness of these things, I have to suffer. I have to suffer and live through it, and then I can appreciate more.

It's why they say that true pleasure does not exist; it's just the temporary release from suffering. Socrates again . . .

CONSCIENCE: *Before the fight against Carlos Condit, I took a few moments to look around me. I was sitting a few feet from the ring. Georges's parents were installed immediately to my left. Behind them was a man in a vintage Manchester United soccer jersey with the number 7 for George Best (clever, I know). Over 17,000 people joined us at the Bell Centre, most of whom would be cheering for Georges. Over to my right was a collection of the world's greatest fighters, from Anderson Silva to Jake Shields. Throngs of film and television stars were there too, wearing their sunglasses at night.*

Before facing Condit, I considered that I was no longer champion. I didn't see myself as the reigning champion. I saw Carlos as the legitimate champion. I hadn't defended my belt for a long time. I saw myself as an aspiring fighter on the path to regaining his title. It delivered a different, *new* kind of joy.

The hardest thing to deal with was the stress of re-entering the ring. Feeling the mat beneath my feet. Hearing the crowd chanting "GSP!" and singing their "*olés.*"

CONSCIENCE: *And then Georges walked in.*

With each of his giant paws on Georges's shoulders, Kristof brought up his pupil to the cage, swatting adoring hands away from Georges's face and shouting constant encouragements. "You will defeat him. You are all-powerful. You will destroy your opponent. You are the champion. This is your time." I know, looking at Kristof's expression, that he means it, and how it is bred in his bones.

The walk ended a few feet in front of me. Georges spoke his final words to his team, looked over at me, paid homage to his handlers, looked over at me again and walked up the stairs into the ring. He was completely alone now, finally, after more than eighteen months away from the fight. Back to his destiny, back to what he does best, back in the world where he most belongs.

It was time for battle.

There is no such thing as a normal friendship in my life. There is no such thing as a normal relationship either. I'm not certain I have *real* friends in the definitive sense of the word. If I am going to reach my goal, I simply cannot afford "normal" relations.

I look at the people who are close to me, the ones I refer to as friends, and I wonder: Will I ever have a relationship like his? Will I ever achieve marriage, children, family? Will I ever own a barbecue or have dishes in my cupboards or live life according to the rules that govern masses of individuals? I look at Rodolphe and his special lady and their dog and their house in the country and their renovations, and I don't see my ideal. I find confusion and misunderstanding.

I have no idea why.

CONSCIENCE: *The first two rounds were a blur of near perfection. I see Georges's training come to life before my eyes. I rediscover him in his element, I recognize signs—the signs of victory, or danger. Just by observing how he controls the center, how good his distance is and how good his pace is—because his early pace will be the same as his final-round pace. He is a machine. Within that first minute, a habituated observer can clearly see if Georges understands his opponent or not. If Georges has figured him out. As time passed by, Georges could deduce that Condit was taking more and more time to think, that his instincts were dissipating. Georges was in his psyche. This is what Georges does best: create doubt during chaos, building expectations of the unexpected. Against Condit, Georges executed the game plan exactly as prescribed. Everything was going as planned—better, even. His knee was an afterthought. The injury no longer existed, it had been banished from my recollection because it no longer mattered. Its time had expired. With each connection against Condit's lanky frame, with each takedown, with every single point scored, Georges was building his lead. He was building control, forcing Condit out of his comfort zone and compelling him, as the fight progressed and time receded, to take risks.*

And then came the third round.

Out of nowhere, as he was apparently losing balance and bending down toward his right, Condit caught Georges at his own game. Georges's eyes followed Condit's head, and he responded with the unexpected. Falling sideways, Condit raised his left leg and pulled his foot back behind his knee. Everybody saw it happening, like a slow-motion re-enactment, like a recurring nightmare. Everybody but Georges. Like a scorpion, Condit recoiled and stung the left side of Georges's head with a vicious kick.

Georges went down, his hands circling, looking for solid ground. His eyes stunned, lost, surprised, checking his bearings. But down he went. The air went out of the building in a single whoosh. Everybody felt it.

Hands covered mouths. Jaws dropped. Spirits fell. Condit pounced.

He pounced on Georges and the fists and elbows and strikes rained from above. It looked like he was connecting with every single blow. Like he was pounding Georges into oblivion. Like we could hear the thud and crunch of each blow. It felt like all other sounds had exited the building. It seemed like not a person in the Bell Centre could believe it. And then, out of the corner of my eye, I saw the man in the George Best jersey rise. With both hands, he pointed to the fighters and screamed, "NOOOOOOO! COME ON GEORGES!!! YOU CAN DO IT! GET UP!! STAND!" His voice broke, but others joined him; he was not alone. A UFC choir improvised in Montreal.

Composed, Georges's mother rose, her hands clasped before her, calmly, like she knew something nobody else did. Georges's dad stood too, but he's where the fight comes from. His hands throwing punches, his head moving, bobbing, dodging blows. Whispering words only his son could hear. Georges was not alone anymore—that's what I think was happening. We were all in there with him, that's what we were trying to do, what we wanted him to know, to feel, to understand. Maybe we couldn't grasp exactly what he was going through, so the only connection possible for us was for him to understand the collective power and energy that lived inside each of us. Support.

And then, somehow, Georges fought back. He kicked at Condit's head from the mat, he rolled and turned and stood. We *all stood with him. He regained his composure. He regained his sense of self, and then he assaulted Condit. He jumped onto him and took him down to the ground and pounded on him. He unleashed the fight of a champion. The will of a victor, of a man with no concern for his own limitations, of a man with regard only for his own possibility. His own way. Less than fifteen minutes later, the referee would raise Georges's hand and confirm him as the only champion in his category.*

He had now climbed the mountain a third time, using a new route, a road never traveled by any other fighter before him. The cornerstone of the foundation of Georges's legacy.

I look at the people I care for, the ones who exist inside my heart, and I shake my head. I don't fully comprehend the lives they lead or the choices they make. Their normal is not my normal, that's for certain. Yet here we are, coexisting and dependent on one another. Achievers.

As I look back, every single person who tried to change me is no longer in my life. All of the people who tried to shape me into something that better represents their idea of a normal existence are gone. My friends are fighters, coaches, managers and agents. They enter my life during training sessions, or when I need to eat or relax. The choice isn't even mine, it's my *routine's*.

There are a select few with whom I go to the movies or a bar. I treasure these occasions, probably because there are so few of them.

My life belongs to me, and I know happiness.

CONSCIENCE: *After the fight and the ring speeches, Georges and the team went back to the dressing room. We were alone in there—his coaches, his security and the medical team. This is when I realized that Georges, above all, is a performer.*

We were in the room and he was getting stitches. He didn't talk about the fight. He didn't mention the title, or the victory, or his record-setting winning streak. The only thing he was interested in, the only thing he wanted to talk about or was remotely curious of, was Condit. He had just fought the man and won a unanimous decision, but he wanted to know one thing: "Did he [Condit] require more stitches than I did, and is he more banged up than I am?" That's it. That's what he said, over and over and over again, forcing the medical staff into a vague yet unsatisfactory answer. The doctor provided responses and platitudes, but it wasn't good enough for Georges. So he asked him again and again. And one more time for good measure. Until one of the meds relented and told Georges he had fewer stitches than Condit: four.

Why does this happen? Georges, at that moment, couldn't remember the entire fight. He didn't yet realize how much he had dominated the other man. The final score—50–45, 49–46 and 50–45—couldn't stand out yet, not for GSP. Right after the fight, the world was a fog, and so was Georges's short-term memory. That's why he asked if Condit looked worse than him. Because it's not enough to have defeated him in the octagon. It's not enough to have regained his world title. It's not enough to have re-emerged after career-threatening knee surgery. Georges needed more than this: like any other fight, he needed to have defeated the man completely. He needed to have beaten him at everything, He required total domination.

Georges's thoughts trick him at moments like these. He was thinking, I got dropped in the third round, I won the fight, and right now I'm getting stitches. That's all he knows. It's all the mind retains, in that moment. Imperfection— another kind of fear, but the same response as usual. Only

later—the next day, when he actually watched his fight—
did Georges realize how well he performed. It's only later
that he realized how, except for fifty-one long seconds of the
third round, he dominated totally.

Aiming to become a great martial artist is a lot like being a
researcher in science or medicine. If you find a remedy for an
ailment, others will profit from it—that's the goal. My goal is to
share all of my learning, all of my knowledge, so that other generations of martial artists will benefit from it. It will raise the bar
and make humans better, smarter, more efficient.

When I am retired from the UFC, I will be able to spend
more time doing this. A true master gives all his knowledge, but
only when the student is ready to receive it. Some students are
not ready for certain teaching. This understanding applies to all
things, I think.

CONSCIENCE: *After backslapping with the team, a five-minute*
shower and those four stitches, Georges put the fancy suit on.
He wanted to look good for the public, he wanted to put on a
good face, but there's one thing that he needed my help with.
He came to me and held his necktie out. "Could you put this
on for me? Please?" That's all he wanted, a bit of help with his
tie. And then we headed to the press conference. Georges faced
the media with a bag of ice against his head. He answered all
of the media's questions.

Outside his octagon performances, these are the moments
when I most admire my friend Georges. After the toughest
war of his career, he answered the same question over and
over and over again. The reporters found new ways of pos-
ing the same question, but Georges never veered from the
first thing he'd answered many months earlier. Sometimes

it causes me to wonder if reporters are even listening to each other's questions. I wonder: Do they read other people's stories? It fascinates me how a half dozen professional sports reporters, one after the other, can pose exactly the same question. I could understand Georges lashing out in frustration, and yet he never does: he just repeats his answer. It's like he's telling them, "You can ask me the same question 150 different ways, it's not going to change my mind, my belief or my response." In many ways, it replicates Georges in the ring: "You can try to hit me with that straight right if you want, but I'm going to take you down to the mat every time."

I wasn't happy immediately after the victory against Condit. I was content to win, but I don't like getting knocked around. It wasn't until I went to my parents' place and watched it with family that I saw what happened.

The postfight feeling of uncertainty is astounding. Watching myself fight, I realize the line between success and failure is so narrow, it's scary. Every single time I win a fight, I better understand how the greater the risk, the greater the reward.

CONSCIENCE: *After meeting the press, with his fancy suit and bag of ice, Georges took me up to a private lounge in the Bell Centre to meet friends and training partners. He still hadn't had a single moment to himself. He posed for pictures, chatted and charmed, and went looking for a bathroom.*

I took him into the hallway, he put his arm around me— for balance as much as brotherly affection—and we walked a few feet to the public loo. "I'm so tired," he said. "And hungry." He stood in front of the mirror and, between shadow and light from the semi-lit sink area, took a good look at himself. He reached up and touched the bridge of his nose. He stroked the side of his swollen cranium. He turned away from the image, shaking his head, and he looked toward me. "Why do I keep doing this to myself?" he said, more a statement than a question. "I don't like this. Everything hurts." Yes, everything hurts, I thought. Yet after a fight, he never takes pain medication. Never.

And then we went to his suite, where a mountain of food from his favorite burger joint was waiting for him. Another key part of his routine . . . pure happiness!

* * *

CONSCIENCE: *Georges and I met on the mat. We rolled. It was a gym in Verdun where I was teaching Brazilian Jiu-Jitsu in 2001.*

The odd truth is that I'm one of his closest and oldest friends, and yet I fucking tolerate a lot of shit from Georges—especially when it's related to a non-training, non-fighting activity. Sometimes—and we can be surrounded by two camera crews and banks of spotlights and backdrops and makeup artists and stylists and hangers-on—Georges just looks at me and I can hear him getting angry. I can sense it, see it in his movements. We catch each other's eye for a split second and I know what's happening in his head. He's pissed. Maybe he's slipped on gelatin left over from a photo shoot and thinks he could hurt something. Maybe he's being asked to take more pictures and it wasn't planned. Maybe some guy keeps sticking a camera right in his face, right there in the ring while he's training. And it's all my fault.

My business partner in our management agency, Phil, is the perfect definition of partner. When Georges stops listening to me, or when a strategic decision must be made, Phil steps in. Together we find solutions to problems I can't solve alone. He covers every angle that I'm blind to. He's every skill I'm not. Georges likes to call Phil "The Brain" (he's a tax lawyer), and when he sees "The Brain" pop up on his smartphone screen, he always answers. Always. Without Phil there with me, none of this would be possible. Nothing. He removes doubt from our decisions. He has the ability to provide unbiased advice that leads to action. Phil, in essence, saves me from my own misery.

* * *

Before the Condit fight, I had to return to St-Isidore for an event at my old high school. On that particular day, I admit that I really didn't want to go. I felt like it was interrupting my pre-fight preparation; we were already in full training-camp mode. Although the timing was not ideal, we drove out to my hometown, I walked into the gymnasium . . . and I saw all those kids before me. I looked into their faces. I met many of them and got to chat for just a few minutes. These young people move me. And by the time we drove away, I understood the importance of having been there. Not just for those kids, but for me personally. They're energizing, inspiring, and they remind me why I have this mission in the first place.

> **CONSCIENCE:** *I understand his stress. I am not naturally a stressed individual, but I am deeply emotional. In French we have an expression, "soupe au lait," which refers to a person who wears his heart on his sleeve. I would say that, as his close friend and manager, I have become hypersensitive to Georges's stress. I know why he's acting weird. This isn't everyday life. And I*

believe that acting this way helps him get ready for the fight, which means it's okay. I understand that real friends can tell each other to fuck off and there's no betrayal. In many ways, I'm privileged: I'm the only person in the world who has this relationship with Georges. He speaks a certain way to me, and I respond in kind . . . People look at us and they can't believe we're friends. But I know that we have the most open and sincere relationship two individuals can have. There is never a word of lie, a lost moment, a lack of clarity. We know better than to try and hide from one another.

It's like children who are too hard on their parents. They speak to them inappropriately, rudely sometimes. Some of us are like that with the people we love. Well, I pick up all that crap when he is stressed. In the entourage, I'm the only one he'll talk to that way. I'm the escape valve—when the pressure gets to be too much, he turns to me. It's funny because Georges, at the start of each training camp, comes to me and says: "Rodolphe, I apologize ahead of time for the next two months. I will be an ass and make your life miserable. I know sometimes I am hard, but I need you and I am sorry." Like I don't already know.

He doesn't need to say these things. It doesn't bother me one bit. My job is not to add to his stress. My job is to absorb his stress. I've never had a job as fulfilling as this one, yet I know he hates everything I do. He always jokes that I have the most boring life in the world, but between the two of us, I'm the one with the extreme job. He sleeps in every day while I need to wake up early, go to meetings, manage the business, manage his life—it makes me laugh.

The irony is that my own personal life is a mess. My bills go unpaid for weeks beyond the deadline while his books are spic and span. My loving girlfriend often sits there on the sofa

or at the table while I spend time on the phone with Georges,
keeping his affairs in order. My renovations are a multi-year
plan, to say the least, but at least they're the source of many
jokes. Yes, his life is ordered and mine is a shambles. Albeit a
happy shambles . . .

This is why I'm here—me and nobody else. Georges
loathes disruption during his training, hates the interrup-
tions that affect rhythm. Every move I make must be stra-
tegic. I won't talk to him during training. I won't discuss
business in the locker room or after his shower. The only
time we can talk about non-fight-related work is when he's
started eating.

But in the lead-up to a fight, I manage everything, and
Georges doesn't even realize it half the time. The schedule for
public appearances, for the UFC events, for his training—
I coordinate all of it. From the cooks to the security, from
dropping and picking up the dry cleaning to making sure the
elevator is there when he's ready to come down, to managing
each room to ensure that the dozens of friends and partners
and sponsors get their tickets to the fight.

I make sure Georges doesn't get up too early in the morn-
ing, so he'll be ready to fight at midnight. I watch for the
media and prep them. I don't let ignorant reporters near him.
Sure, I'll coach "uneducated" reporters, but later, not during
training before a fight. I screen every single person who'll
interview Georges: Who is he/she? Does he/she know MMA?
Has he/she been to one of these before? Does he/she know his
stuff? I do all of the due diligence because we can't afford to
waste our time. We can't afford to have a reporter address
him as Nick because he doesn't know the difference between
Georges St-Pierre and Nick Diaz (I am not making this up).
But I do this because I love it; it puts me in my element and

lets me invent the environment I think works best to meet our goals.

Georges hates public training sessions and he doesn't want to do them. But for his career, he has to allow them, and sometimes for the UFC promos I find alternatives. He shows up and signs giveaway DVDs and T-shirts. He shakes hands and meets his fans. He likes meeting fans and taking pictures with them. He likes to ask about their day and what they do. These are small, stupid details, but together they make up the bigger picture.

In fact, the most important thing is to be able to stick to the schedule because Georges will probably have booked two additional training sessions before and after the lunch break, and we need to find a way to be on time.

We've had documentary filmmakers in the room before fights, and I make all the cameramen wear UFC T-shirts so they'll disappear in the familiar fog of commonality that exists in Georges's head. I create and manage Georges's environment, like an orchestra leader. The truth is that Georges didn't know he was being filmed by a documentary crew the day he fought Condit. I didn't want to tell him. I couldn't risk a temporary loss of focus or momentary frustration. I wouldn't change the prefight picture that exists in his mind. I told the cameraman to look down or away if Georges even gazed in his direction. "Do not speak," I added, "because he'll know you're not from the UFC. Get out of his face, because twenty seconds of inattention means you're bothering Georges." At the end of the day, the film's not the priority—the fight is.

These are just details, but I've always treated small matters with great attention; it pre-empts matters of great concern . . . and I've known the ins and outs of my friend Georges for so long now. Nothing Georges does is normal. Nobody in his entourage is normal. He and I are always fighting, like an old couple. What's more, he thinks I'm the weird one. He doesn't understand our "normal" lives, and how we go through every single day doing things we don't want to do. He doesn't do anything he doesn't want to do, except for the occasional photo shoot, but he does that because it's all part of the plan. His favorite photo session of all time was a fashion shoot—we timed it and it took five minutes and forty-one seconds. The photographer from that day gets to shoot Georges more often now . . .

To become champion and do what Georges does, a great part of his life is egocentric. It has to be. When to train, when and what to eat, what to do and why: these are the priorities, and they can't ever come second. He must come first, before anything or anybody else. It's the only way he can have any hope of reaching his goals. Georges will never tolerate someone who tries to carve out a place in his life while bringing about change that is unrelated to his greater goal. He can't. He won't. His goal is to become the greatest martial artist of all time. Nothing can take away from his focus. People coming in and out of his life can't halt or slow the process. They won't last.

Georges wants to change the sport. He seeks to bring it to a new level. It's his vocation. His destination. Every single person who tried to stray from that ideal is gone.

We were visiting a school, and a little boy wanted to ask me a question about bullying. I recognized my ten-year-old self in his body language. He sat there, slouched forward, head down, his voice a frightened whisper. So I interrupted him mid-sentence. I asked him to stand up and roll his shoulders back. I asked him to look me straight in the eye and speak up so that I, and everyone else, could hear his question. And he did. He sounded great, and what a smile he had. I think about him all the time.

CONSCIENCE: *There's more than just the technical perspective to how Georges wishes to become the greatest martial artist of all time. It won't happen exclusively inside the octagon, or be limited to performing various martial arts in dojos or wats or boxing clubs. In this new era of communications, Georges must also rely on all the tools at his disposal to fulfill his mission. It's why he has developed his brand and his communications platforms. He has his own media channels on You-Tube, Facebook and Twitter. He works with sponsors. He's spearheading a new wave of professional athletes who want to develop links with fans using social media. He's trying to bring himself, and his sport, to new levels—and it seems to have worked so far. He wears suits for many public appearances, and now other fighters have to do it. His "branding" has helped the UFC image and has brought new sponsors to the table. It has attracted new fans to the sport and has opened minds about UFC fighters. Georges has found an innovative way of highlighting the facts about mixed martial arts and challenged conventional thinking and stigma related to violence.*

While Georges now has devoted Canadian and U.S. agents and a global marketing firm behind him, most people don't know that Georges built the foundation of his brand all by himself. Before anyone started working on his marketing channels, Georges's brand was good and well because he doesn't know any other way to act than to be genuine. Not once has he veered from his own legitimacy, from his own truth, from the best way to tell his story. All the marketing angles are based on it, inspired by it, and limited to it. I remember the instructions he gave us when the sponsorships started growing: "Just make sure everything stays 100-percent authentic—it's the only thing I insist on," he said. "No bullshit."

Nothing really frustrates me to the point of hatred. It's not worth the energy. I don't like people who are super slow. Everything happens in my mind at the same speed as my training. That's why I expect my team to always be prepared for our meetings. There is no time to waste. I like to go from the introduction to the conclusion fast, and then decide.

CONSCIENCE: *Georges can't think of his future outside the UFC right now; his focus can't allow him to. He doesn't know what he wants to do yet after his fighting career. Our team's job is to give him options and prepare the next steps. We've already started looking at the design of a martial arts academy where Georges would teach youth.*

Seven days before the fight, Georges and his tight-knit entourage move into a hotel suite to get ready for the main event. The main room in the suite becomes a dining room and common area. It's where everybody meets because everybody has free access, it's where the TV is, and it's where the food is served. There are Georges, myself, Kristof, Firas, John and Eddy, his personal security guard and friend. The bedrooms are adjacent to the main room. The week before the fight is quite uneventful because Georges is cutting weight. We watch films, documentaries, anything to take our minds off the upcoming fight. Before the Condit fight, we watched a lot of animals fighting. There was this one great documentary about lions attacking hyenas. We always watch a few of the same mindless films, knowing they'll make everybody laugh and give Georges a reprieve.

In the eighteen months before Georges won his title against Condit, we lived on a cloud. We were signing sponsorship deals; in fact, we signed at least three times as many as usual because he was inactive (and had time to do it). The real world of the octagon and the fight seemed so far away from us, an intangible we couldn't fathom. We could look down from the cloud and know that someday we'd be back in the real world, but it seemed like a distant journey. And then, all of a sudden, we weren't on the cloud anymore. We were fighting. We were back in the warrior mindset, aware that in the fighting world, you're no better than your last performance. To have eighteen months to sell a world champion is a heck of an opportunity, a dream for any manager.

The UFC title is, in my opinion, the hardest championship to hold on to. The system is unique and no other sport replicates it: as champ, you are always facing the second-best fighter in the world. In boxing, the champion gets to pick two of his upcoming opponents until the third fight, the big title defense. This is when the federations impose a choice on you. Not so much in the UFC. In the UFC, you're always fighting the number-two contender. It's not up to you. You don't have a choice. Georges is always imposed on the top guy. There are no breaks.

I take no painkillers after the fight. I don't need them.

The Wednesday after the Condit fight—three days later—I went back to training.

EPILOGUE

I'm really just a normal person.

know that some of the things I do are different from the traditional norm, but when it comes down to basics, I'm like anybody else. I have my good days and not-so-good days. I told the audiences at Cannes that the big secret to my success in accruing a big support system has been to simply be myself, something that has been enthusiastically supported by members of my immediate community.

I've written in these pages about hiring to my weaknesses, and it's a theme that keeps coming up in my life because I keep finding things I could be better at. I either hire people to help me become better at my profession—like Phil Nurse with Muay Thai—or, as I play a very visible role in a very visible industry and want to create the best impression on young people who may be having similar childhood experiences to mine, I work with experts who fill needed outreach areas like developing a website and Facebook page.

The only way for me to determine success—to evaluate whether or not an outside "thing" is going well—is to know myself and know if I'm acquitting myself genuinely. As I said, prior to the Koscheck fight, Josh hyped the fight by trash-talking. Coming from me, it would have sounded strange—or at least it would have been uncomfortable. I have to know myself and understand what works for me and what doesn't. This is why I always seek coaches from other disciplines, other countries—to broaden my knowledge. It's also why I created an expert team for everything that happens *outside* the octagon. But while I seek to surround myself with experts, I also distinctly look for those who are like-minded. And to assess like-minded individuals, I have to first know who *I* am. What *I* believe. How *I* think. And what *I* feel.

Firas and I discuss this all the time.

"I could hardly know anything else if I did not even know myself." Socrates said that, and the way I understand it, a person has to truly know himself before he can start even considering understanding the rest of society. Self-examination gives you a base to work from, and then you can tackle bigger questions.

One of the keys to learning for me has been to not get so hung up on the past. It's important to remember the past, but that doesn't mean you have to torture yourself with it by reliving it every single day. Once I got over my anger and rage from childhood, once I stopped feeling like a victim, I was able to open myself to great sources of learning. I had to channel that part of my life, especially the emotional recovery, as I dealt with an injury that has traditionally been the bane of competitive athletes across disciplines.

I am only thirty-one years old as I write this story, but it's entirely possible that in five or ten years, my outlook will have changed on many of the things that have been discussed herein. Maybe I'll have the same core beliefs but have more vivid illustrations to describe them. No doubt, with age, I'll *feel* differently, which most certainly affects everyone's outlook. I'm cognizant that the goal for me over time will be to vary my regimen according to my personal goals and, of course, my aging body's individual requirements. Once I hang up my hand wraps for the final time as an MMA competitor, I'll have to find another path to follow. But even though I can't fight forever, movement is my life force, and I'll use the experience of my recent rehabilitation—which made this book possible—to keep questioning things, to learn more about myself and the world.

Progress, I've learned, comes from openness.

Acknowledgments

Many thanks are in order: To my mom and dad, for recalling stories from my childhood home. To my coaches Kristof Midoux, John Danaher and Firas Zahabi, for playing such a big role in my life, inside and outside the octagon. To all my coaches and training partners over the years, too many to list here. To my Canadian agents, Rod Beaulieu and Phil Lepage, and my U.S. agents at Creative Artists Agency, with a special nod to Nez Balelo, Mike Fonseca and Simon Green. To my editor Adam Korn, whose leadership elevated the contents of this book. To my friend Justin Kingsley and researcher Guinness "Smed" Rider, for their patience and hard work on this project. And a special thanks to all of my fans, for always being there for me.